Financial Engineering
of Climate Investment in
Developing Countries

ANTHEM ENVIRONMENT AND SUSTAINABILITY

General Editor: Lawrence Susskind – Massachusetts Institute of Technology (MIT), USA

Our Environment and Sustainability book publishing program seeks to push the frontiers of scholarship while simultaneously offering prescriptive and programmatic advice to policymakers and practitioners around the world. We have launched this initiative with the series below (each of which has an excellent editorial board featuring scholars, practitioners and business experts eager to link theory and practice), and will continue it with research monographs, professional and major reference works, upper-level textbooks and general interest titles.

Another related project to the Anthem Environment and Sustainability program is Anthem EnviroExperts Review. Through this online micro-reviews site, Anthem Press seeks to build a community of practice involving scientists, policy analysts and activists that is committed to creating a clearer and deeper understanding of how ecological systems – at every level – operate, and how they have been damaged by unsustainable development. We seek to publish on this site short reviews of all important books or reports in the environmental field, broadly defined. For more information, visit www.anthemenviroexperts.com.

Related Series

Anthem Advances in Atmospheric Environment Science
Deepening our understanding of atmospheric sciences and the social and political implications of regulatory efforts that build on them. Series Editors: Peter Brimblecombe – University of East Anglia, UK and Ranjeet S. Sokhi – University of Hertfordshire, UK

Anthem Ecosystem Services and Restoration Series
Understanding ecosystem services and harnessing market forces to drive conservation and restoration. Series Editor: Lawrence Susskind – MIT, USA

Anthem New Energy Finance
Encouraging productive public and private investments in a low-carbon future. Series Editor: Nicholas Howarth – The Smith School of Enterprise and the Environment, University of Oxford, UK

Anthem Series on International Environmental Policy and Agreements
Building a prescriptive environmental policymaking agenda based on sound analysis and empirical insights. Series Editor: Saleem H. Ali – University of Queensland, Australia

Anthem Sustainability and Risk Series
Improving our ability to promote sustainable development in the context of increasing complexity, uncertainty and risk. Series Editor: David A. Wirth – Boston College Law School, USA

Anthem Sustainability Science
Documenting our ability to promote sustainability development. Series Editor: William Moomaw – Tufts University, USA

Anthem Water Diplomacy Series
Enhancing our understanding of better ways to facilitate the management of shared water resources at international and national levels. Series Editor: Shafiqul Islam – Tufts University, USA

Financial Engineering of Climate Investment in Developing Countries

Nationally Appropriate Mitigation Action and How to Finance It

Søren E. Lütken

ANTHEM PRESS
LONDON · NEW YORK · DELHI

Anthem Press
An imprint of Wimbledon Publishing Company
www.anthempress.com

This edition first published in UK and USA 2015
by ANTHEM PRESS
75–76 Blackfriars Road, London SE1 8HA, UK
or PO Box 9779, London SW19 7ZG, UK
and
244 Madison Ave #116, New York, NY 10016, USA

First published in hardback by Anthem Press in 2014

British Library Cataloguing-in-Publication Data
A catalogue record for this book is available from the British Library.

Library of Congress Cataloging-in-Publication Data
The Library of Congress has cataloged the hardcover edition as follows:
Lütken, Søren Ender, author.
Financial engineering of climate investment in developing countries
: Nationally Appropriate Mitigation Action and how to finance it /
Søren E. Lütken.
pages cm. – (Anthem environment and sustainability)
Includes bibliographical references and index.
ISBN-13: 978-1-78308-018-2 (hardcover : alk. paper)
ISBN-10: 1-78308-018-3 (hardcover : alk. papre)
1. Greenhouse gas mitigation–Economic aspects–Developing
countries. 2. Climate change mitigation–Government
policy–Developing countries. 3. Climatic changes–Economic
aspects–Developing countries. I. Title.
TD885.5.G73L88 2014
363.738'746091724–dc23
2014008273
9781783084272

ISBN-13: 978 1 78308 427 2 (Pbk)
ISBN-10: 1 78308 427 8 (Pbk)

This title is also available as an ebook.

CONTENTS

List of Figures and Tables   ix
List of Abbreviations   xi
Foreword   xiii
Preface   xv

Chapter 1   Introduction   **1**

Part I   What Is

**Chapter 2   Climate Change and Nationally Appropriate
               Mitigation Action**   **9**
The Identity of a NAMA   10
PoAs and NAMAs   15
Defining Appropriateness   16
The Substance of NAMAs   20
Summing Up   24

Chapter 3   Learning from the CDM   **25**
The CDM Experience   26
   It's a market – live with it   28
   Thriving on domestic finance   29
   Small is beautiful …   30
   Cost *in*efficient emissions reduction   31
   Additionality revisited   33
   Reverse engineering the CDM   34
Summing Up   37

Chapter 4   Defining NAMA Finance   **39**
Government Investment Motives   44
Private Investment Motives   46
Summing Up   48

Chapter 5   The Financing Tools . . .   **51**
Public Sector Sourcing Instruments   54
Environmental Fiscal Reform   55
　Non-domestic sources   59
Public Sector Operational Instruments   59
　Grants   59
　Taxes   60
　Loans and guarantees   61
　What happened to the carbon credit?   62
Summing Up   65

Chapter 6   . . . And the Financiers   **67**
The Intitutional Investor   70
The Insurance Companies   72
Hybrid Sources of Financing   74
　The philanthropic foundation trustees   75
The Banks   76
　Multilateral development banks   76
　National development banks   77
Green Bonds   77
Blending   79
Summing Up   80

Chapter 7   Engineering and Leveraging the Finance   **81**
Transformation   83
Leveraging Finance from Different Sources   84
　The 'who goes first' dilemma   85
　Additional domestic public funding   86
　Approaching international financiers   88
　Engaging the local private sector   89
　Attracting Foreign Direct Investment (FDI)   91
The Right Order of Leveraging   92
Summing Up   97

Part II   What Ought to Be

Chapter 8   Challenges to NAMA Finance – Mandates,
**　　　　　　Aggregation and Lack of Instruments**   **101**
The Aggregation Gap   102
　The guarantee system and its shortcomings   105
　The ECAs as aggregators   109

Mandates   110
Summing Up   115

Chapter 9   Roles of the Green Climate Fund   **117**
The Green Climate Fund and Risk   120
The Green Climate Fund and Green Bonds   122
The Green Climate Fund and Equity   126
The Green Climate Fund as Aggregator   129
Other Options   130
Putting the Pieces Together   133
Summing Up   134

Chapter 10   Conclusion   **137**
How to Start?   141

Notes   143
References   147
Index   149

LIST OF FIGURES AND TABLES

Figures

Figure 1.   NAMAs in the context of general
             development planning   19
Figure 2.   Weight of policy versus project NAMAs
             relative to capabilities of developing countries   22
Figure 3.   Emissions reduction returns on investment in the CDM   32
Figure 4.   From ex-post to ex-ante approvals in CDM   36
Figure 5.   Financial engineering of NAMAs   44
Figure 6.   Sub-optimal investments in emissions reduction   46
Figure 7.   Multilateral investment in mitigation
             and typical instruments employed   53
Figure 8.   Sourcing instruments and operational
             instruments for NAMA financing   55
Figure 9.   Direct and indirect taxation   57
Figure 10.   Cost of types of risk   63
Figure 11.   The right order of leveraging   86
Figure 12.   The financing value chain   94
Figure 13.   Instruments in the financing value chain   95
Figure 14.   Maximizing leveraging   96
Figure 15.   The aggregators' central role in organizing financing   104
Figure 16   Expanded securitization model   119
Figure 17.   Simple investment structure involving green bonds   126
Figure 18.   Options for financial product development   133

Table

Table 1. Types of Policy NAMAs   21

LIST OF ABBREVIATIONS

BAU	Business as Usual
CDM	Clean Development Mechanism
CER	Certified Emission Reductions
CIF	Climate Investment Fund
COP	Conference of the Parties, followed by a number that refers to the vintage of the meeting, e.g. COP17, COP18, COP19
DAC	Development Assistance Committee (of the OECD)
ECA	Export Credit Agency
ESCO	Energy Service Company
ETS	Emission Trading Systems
FDI	Foreign Direct Investment
GCF	Green Climate Fund
GEF	Global Environment Facility
ICA	International Consultation and Analysis (of unilateral NAMAs)
IDA	International Development Agency
IPCC	Intergovernmental Panel on Climate Change
LCDS	Low Carbon Development Strategy
LDC	Least Developed Countries (according to the UN)
LEDS	Low Emission Development Strategies
MRI	Mission Related Investment
MRV	Measurement, Reporting and Verification
NAMA	Nationally Appropriate Mitigation Action 'official' guidance used as reference for the NAMA guide published by UNFCCC, UNDP and UNEP in 2013, see references (UNFCCC, UNDP, UNEP 2013)
OECD	Organisation for Economic Co-operation and Development
PEBBLE	Pan European Bank to Bond Loan Equitization
PMR	Partnership for Market Readiness (World Bank)
PoA	Programme of Activity (under the CDM)
TNA	Technology Needs Assessment
Unilateral	No financial support from other countries
UNFCCC	United Nations Framework Convention on Climate Change
VCS	Voluntary Carbon Standard
WB	World Bank

FOREWORD

As a pioneer in mainstream climate finance, I have spent years trying to understand how and where finance can play a role in more environmentally friendly business solutions. To understand this, an understanding of both science and finance is needed, and consequently it is tough to get a full overview. In a time where we all know that pollution is a challenge, both for city environments and chemical balances in the atmosphere, it is of high importance to identify, understand and list potential solutions. The work done by Dr Lütken to support this process by writing this book is therefore of very high importance and I strongly commend and recommend this book.

Christopher Flensborg
Head of Sustainable Products and
Product Development, SEB

PREFACE

There is a long-standing problem with the international negotiations, which should have delivered a response to the climate challenge many years ago. While the changing climate will affect us all eventually, we tend to tackle it as a political problem primarily, rather than a practical challenge that needs practical solutions from practical people. The negotiations are elitarian, strategic and non-inclusive, existing in their own sphere, leaving all other stakeholders – and we are, in essence, all stakeholders – in separate parallel spheres. These spheres only occasionally collide or interact. When they do, negotiators realize that they do not speak the same language; the interaction is fruitless. The results, in practice, are few and far between – and certainly have not yielded any useful answers yet. Or have they?

Over the 20 years that climate change negotiations have been ongoing, the developing countries as a group have become by far the largest emitter, while greenhouse gas emissions in developed countries are falling, albeit so far marginally. The Nationally Appropriate Mitigation Action (NAMA) is the new kid on the block in the battle against climate change, which is supposed to bring the emissions in developing countries under control. Without it, any attempt to reverse global emission trends will be in vain. Building on 10 years of experience with the Clean Development Mechanism (CDM), NAMAs are about to find their own identity and, most importantly, find a new financial basis without addressing an international carbon market and without thriving on a carbon credit. This book gives the first no-nonsense, hands-on account of the financing principles and prospects for NAMAs, unravelling the nature of the NAMA, which to most remain mysterious. The mystery, however, is not a result of convoluted formulations or complicated rule-sets, but due to the absence of such formulations. As such, the NAMA is in a regulatory vacuum in stark contrast to what has led the CDM to become a regulatory nightmare.

Nevertheless, while the NAMA may be the right instrument at the right time, the challenge is that it is spawned from the negotiation sphere, deployed without much interaction with other spheres. Therefore, there is a barrier between concept and action – the realization of which is growing by the day.

The disconnect is, first and foremost, between the political sphere and the private sector sphere – particularly the financial aspect of it. Moreover, there is a persistent language problem.

In addition to the serious problems caused by the different languages spoken in the parallel spheres there is also a slightly smaller concern as to the choice of language for this book. Obviously the intended readers, given the subject of 'NAMA and financing', are per definition representatives of both spheres. Attempting to bridge the language divide has unavoidable consequences. If it is to be readable for all parties, the book must avoid becoming very technical – which, consequently, it is not. The flipside of that coin, however, is that the experts from either sphere may find their subject treated superficially and with lacking nuance. I apologize for that. Notwithstanding this compromise, the result should be a book that is a relatively easy read for all that are interested in greenhouse gas mitigation in developing countries and are concerned with how to make that happen.

I sincerely thank my long time mentor Karl-Heinz Schulz, first, for inspiring me to start writing the book and, second, for his invaluable contributions to the risk sections of the book. Having worked together in the past on risk products, and for the carbon market through the Danish Export Credit Agency (which, as far as it is known, remains the only agency to offer dedicated carbon market risk products), it was natural to take this collaboration further to the NAMA.

I also thank my employer, the UNEP Risø Centre, for providing the knowledge platform for NAMAs, from which I write. I wish to emphasize that the messages and viewpoints conveyed in this book are solely my personal views and interpretations. The UNEP Risø Centre cannot, in any way, be held responsible.

It is my hope that this modest contribution to the discourse on climate finance will help parties in all spheres understand the NAMA and the financing platforms that will help them materialize, and, if possible, also help people in different spheres of the climate political firmament understand each other.

Søren E. Lütken
January 2014

Chapter 1

INTRODUCTION

The climatic consequences of the way we live may be the greatest challenge humanity has ever faced. The challenge does not necessarily lie in the immense actions that need to be concerted to confront it, but rather in how difficult it is to grasp. Although by now most have realized that something is wrong with the weather, the real consequences of the dramatic shifts in the climate, which are being warned against by climate scientists in ever more alarming phrasing, still seem like science fiction. Moreover, while we can calculate – and have calculated – the cost of inaction, and realize that it may be cheaper to prevent the problem, we are much better at accommodating the costs of natural disasters that require immediate relief, rather than replacing perfectly functional, even brilliantly engineered, technology that just is not compatible with a zero-emission future. In all likelihood, therefore, we may have to depend on our eminent adaptation skills when faced with the clear and present dangers – dangers that will only become clearer as emissions continue to grow.

Structured negotiations on meeting the climate challenge have been on-going since 1992. Compared to the amount of time it has taken to build the carbon-based economy, that is not very long – particularly when considering that what is fundamentally being negotiated is the dismantling of this carbon-based economy. With hydrocarbons deeply entrenched in the economic system, and promises of wealth still embedded in exploration in a growing number of developing countries, having 200 countries arrive at a consensus to forego such promises of wealth takes more than a science-fiction-like warning.

In this respect, negotiations have brought about a rather swift pricing of carbon emissions. The Kyoto Protocol in 1997 managed to set a cap on emissions, however limited, and allowed trading in emission allowances, thus effectively taxing hydrocarbons. The flagship of the Kyoto Protocol, the Clean Development Mechanism (CDM), even brought the carbon price to developing economies promising rents from developed countries' carbon market if emissions were reduced on a project-by-project basis. Project-based carbon accounting systems were established, trading models were developed, and a whole new industry was created in the process. In those 17 short years the global challenge was faced, a global architecture was established, a market mechanism was developed and operated – and wrecked. The CDM and the market that supported it rose and fell in a matter of 10 years. The carbon market crashed in 2012 for a number of reasons, including the international financial crisis, the expiry of the Kyoto Protocol's first commitment period, and because the Protocol's relevance had been eroded by global economic development. At its expiry, less than 13 per cent of global greenhouse gas emissions were under the constraint of the Protocol. Whatever the replacement emerging from negotiations, it will have to address expectations that a much larger share of global emissions have to come under some sort of constraint.

Attempts to establish a replacement for the Kyoto Protocol have been on-going in international climate negotiations for years, so far with astonishingly little progress in lieu of the calamities in store for humanity, and life on Earth as a whole, if the current emission trends are allowed to continue unrestrained. One of the founding principles of the Framework Convention is the division of labour expressed as 'common but differentiated responsibilities'. In short that means that developed countries should take the lead in mitigation efforts, assisting developing countries with technology, finance and capacity building to enable them to do their part while leaving sufficient room, in emission terms, for their continued development. During those negotiations, developed countries as a whole were still the larger emitter, but the balance has shifted rapidly leaving the developing economies as the largest emitter by far.

In May 2013 the concentration of carbon dioxide in the atmosphere reached 400 parts per million (ppm).[1] This number was the first possible target mentioned as a desirable stabilization level for greenhouse gas concentration in the atmosphere during initial negotiations in the beginning of the 1990s, but was raised to 450 ppm. This increase is still somewhat compatible with the ambition – internationally agreed upon since 2010 – of keeping the average global temperature increase below 2 degrees centigrade as 450 ppm leaves about 50 per cent chance of meeting the target (see, e.g., OECD Environmental Outlook to 2050 (2011)). Currently, the average annual increase is about 2 ppm. By a layman's simple calculation this would give all the countries of the world 25 years to keep emitting carbon dioxide – and then after that stop entirely! There are many more advanced, and correct, ways of presenting these calculations – none of which improve the prospects of meeting the challenge.

The luxury of time enjoyed in the early days of climate change negotiations is over. The division of labour has ebbed out, slowly eroding the division between developed and developing countries' obligations – a division that in any case was more on paper than in action when observing the enormous renewable energy investments undertaken in many developing and transitional economies and how much emissions have been outsourced from developed economies into the unaccounted-for emissions accounts of low cost manufacturing regimes[2].

While these equalizing trends were greatly unintended during the drafting of the Convention and the Protocol, an intended equalization has slowly found its way into negotiation texts. This intention has been on the part of developed country parties that are increasingly realizing that whatever effort they might agree to would be in vain unless the rapidly growing economies in Asia and Latin America would constrain their growth in emissions – and begin to reduce these emissions in the near future. The fact is that from 1990 to 2010, the developed countries listed in Annex 1 to the UNFCCC reduced their emissions from 19 to 17 gigatonnes of CO_2 equivalents (reasons untold), whereas the developing countries increased their emissions from 16 to 31 gigatonnes. Consequently, they became the source of the global increase in greenhouse gas emissions by 58 per cent over the 20 year period that preferably should have seen a change in the trend.

These simple yet alarming statistics are at odds with traditional development objectives. Suddenly, the 'development first' principle seems somewhat shortsighted. Unless the trends in emissions are changed dramatically in the short term there may not be much development to speak of at all, and trends would need to change dramatically in developing countries.

It is not that the developed countries are off the hook. They still need to cut their emissions ambitiously – to the tune of 80 per cent by 2050 according to the UNEP emissions gap report 2013 (UNEP 2013). But the figures underscore the urgency of addressing the spiralling emissions from countries in transition and practically all others, maybe with the exemption of countries least developed. Inventing the term of 'Nationally Appropriate Mitigation Action' to frame efforts in 'non-Annex-1' countries for relative emissions reduction is therefore highly appropriate in itself – even timely if looking at traditional dynamics of international negotiations.

The Nationally Appropriate Mitigation Actions (NAMAs) represents a major shift in approach to the division of responsibility. It brings net emissions reduction in developing countries into the global climate change regime architecture, without an international offsetting mechanism, like the CDM, through which any emissions reduction achieved in a developing country would be countered by a similar increase in emissions in a developed country. The NAMA concept, therefore, is not only appropriate in a national context for developing countries, it is also very appropriate internationally.

Bringing the NAMA from concept to implementation, however, has its challenges. Many of these challenges originate in current financing structures, in the entrenchment of the carbon economy, and in the fact that most lower emissions alternatives come at a cost higher than the hydrocarbon alternative. Financial engineering of NAMAs will not change this; thus it is not about making the cost disappear – it is about mobilizing the will to entertain it. This can be done by making the cost look more appealing – by reducing it, shifting the burden among parties, aligning payments with other benefits, reducing risks, increasing payback times, and dozens of other means – even to the point of finding 'free' funds.

Of course there is always the promise of continuously falling prices on emission free technology that ultimately will turn these alternatives into the preferred economic choice. In such cases the financial engineering may contribute to their competitiveness – or the hope, from a climate protection perspective, that the concept of 'unburnable carbon' takes root and significantly drives up oil and coal prices. In the meantime, however, the financial engineering of NAMAs is an indispensable discipline, if these mitigation actions are to make any dent in the rapidly growing emissions in developing countries.

This book uses the term 'financial engineering', which is a field normally taught at business schools for people with aspirations in investment banking. It includes tools like swaps and derivatives, options and repo market strategies and a host of other techniques, which are not addressed in this book. There are many books and courses serving this segment. The term 'financial engineering' is used in this context for the financing principles, which can materialize the billions of investment dollars that would be needed in the coming years in response to the climate challenge – increasingly so in developing countries. The NAMA is the new concept that can make this happen, and the financial engineering of NAMAs is what will help developing countries deliver an adequate response.

This book is not rich in formulas and calculations, but rather focuses on the instruments available for the promotion and structuring of public and private economic interaction. It is realistic in the sense that it illustrates what does and does not have prospects, while also including concepts and ideas that are imported from other areas of finance. It has an implicit focus on leveraging, which is currently the preferred term to illustrate public–private interaction (despite its connotations of 'us' and 'them' as opposed to a more collaborative effort), as well as on the dual meaning of 'leveraged funds', depending on whether the funds are leveraged from the private or public sector.

Importantly, the focus of this book is on the financing of the NAMA – not on the financing of the *preparation* of the NAMA. The technical assistance is left out in this regard, partly because it is already an on-going activity rapidly on the rise in the donor community, and also because there is not much engineering in the provision of a grant. Furthermore, it is not the technical capacity that reduces emissions; it is the investments in physical assets with a low emission profile.

It is perhaps due to the focus on technical assistance that many NAMAs are being developed without much concern for their financial basis. Most NAMA guides treat finance as an afterthought, and not as a planning and structuring tool. However, developing the skill to write a NAMA proposal is not the same as pulling together financiers in a financing model that is *not* a grant. Instead, it requires a model that includes both public and private sources and instruments, addressing asset financing and operational costs. Without the understanding and acceptance, from the outset, that the chosen financial model is as much the identity of the NAMA as its technology focus or its link to national development policies, many NAMAs are likely to remain project proposals with little chance of materialization. The dialogue between the traditionally separate spheres of climate policy development and project finance needs to commence at the beginning of NAMA development, not at the end.

Part I
WHAT IS

Chapter 2

CLIMATE CHANGE AND NATIONALLY APPROPRIATE MITIGATION ACTION

The Nationally Appropriate Mitigation Action, or NAMA as it has come to be known, first appeared at the 13th Conference of the Parties to the UNFCCC in Bali, Indonesia, in 2007. Prior to it were the coining of the fundamental 'common but differentiated responsibility' principle in 1992 in the Climate Change Convention;[1] its reconfirmation in the Kyoto Protocol in 1997; the operationalization of the Protocol in Marrakech in 2001, and the entering into force of the Protocol just two years earlier in 2005.

The first steps to moving away from this division of labour were taken with the Bali Roadmap, which launched a new process to enhance implementation of the Convention that stipulated a return to 1990 levels of greenhouse gas emissions by 2000. The Kyoto Protocol revised this for developed countries reducing 'their overall emissions of greenhouse gases by at least 5 per cent below 1990 levels in the commitment period 2008 to 2012' – a target that, despite all controversy about insufficient action, in fact has been achieved. The Bali Action Plan (UNFCCC, 2007) states that in order to 'Enhance national/ international action on mitigation of climate change', developing countries will take 'Nationally appropriate mitigation actions … in the context of sustainable development, supported and enabled by technology, financing and capacity-building, in a measurable, reportable and verifiable manner'. This is the first mention of the Nationally Appropriate Mitigation Actions (NAMAs) in the international climate change negotiations. From here the concept has evolved, slowly. By 2010, differentiation between internationally supported actions and unilateral actions, for the first time, stipulated that 'developing country Parties will take nationally appropriate mitigation actions … aimed at achieving a deviation in emissions relative to 'business as usual' emissions in 2020 through own initiative and employing their own financial means.'

The 2010 Cancun Agreements establish that 'developed country Parties shall provide enhanced financial, technological and capacity building support for the preparation and implementation of nationally appropriate mitigation actions of developing country Parties' (UNFCCC, 2010). Cancun also established the Green Climate Fund (GCF) as a vehicle for deploying USD 100 billion per year by 2020 mobilized from developed countries to finance mitigation and adaptation actions in developing countries. The figure stemmed from a speech given in June 2009 by then British Prime Minister Gordon Brown in the run-up to the high-profile 15th Conference of the Parties in Copenhagen later that year – at which 100+ state leaders blatantly failed to produce the highly anticipated global climate deal.

From a negotiations perspective incremental progress has been achieved in Durban at COP17 with the Durban Platform being established eroding some of the divisions between developed and developing countries in terms of emissions reduction, and in Doha at COP18, where Parties agreed to establish a work programme to understand the diversity of NAMAs, only to achieve practically nothing in Warsaw at COP19.

The Identity of a NAMA

Over the past decade, investment bankers have had to come to terms with the Clean Development Mechanism, which was a product – eventually the flagship – of the Kyoto Protocol. Very few bankers took up the challenge of familiarizing themselves with the mechanism; the few that did embraced it as an addition to the financial landscape, while most embarked on emissions trading, buying Certified Emissions Reductions (CERs) from such CDM projects and on-selling these carbon offsets mainly in the European Emission Trading System.

Meanwhile, the 'climate community' consisting of development professionals in a multitude of roles have promoted the mechanism as a climate finance instrument without much interaction with the finance sector, and without much willingness to perform any reality check of the mechanism's actual functionality – which will be addressed in the following chapter. Moreover, in the middle of the development professionals and the bankers, there has been a consulting sector that has equally promoted the mechanism. This has been mostly for the business opportunities it offers, in terms of production of documentation needed for registration of projects under the CDM, which allow the projects to generate CERs.

These three groups of professionals have had to realize that the CDM is fading. The NAMA has eclipsed the CDM in grant programmes and in technical assistance provided to potential NAMA host countries where there is an awareness about financing opportunities related to climate policy development and implementation.

Bankers who previously considered the CDM are now wondering if the NAMA is something they should devote their attention to, while consultants are trying their best to turn the NAMA into something akin to the CDM, by promoting NAMA crediting mechanisms – and, thus, business opportunities related to documentation. Also, the development professionals and climate change negotiators are trying to come to terms with what was actually meant when the NAMA was coined in the Bali Action Plan in 2007.

Some of the NAMA definition has already been established by way of a joint publication produced by the UNFCCC, UNDP and UNEP Risø and launched at COP19 in Warsaw in 2013 (UNFCCC, UNDP, UNEP Risø, 2013). The definitions provided in that publication have been useful in what follows. Although it does not claim to be the 'official guidance' to NAMAs, it will be labelled as such from this point forth, for ease of reference.

A fundamental difference between the CDM and the NAMA is that the NAMA is a concept, not a mechanism. This may be the main reason for the widespread bewilderment that surrounds the NAMA. While the CDM has brought about a regulatory environment developed in the minutest detail, the NAMA has not. Moreover, it is becoming increasingly apparent that it is not going to – making the CDM and the NAMA fundamentally different. However, what distinguishes a NAMA from a project activity under the CDM is, primarily, the context.

NAMAs hold the promise of scaled-up mitigation efforts in developing countries freed from the rigorous CDM requirements and the constraints of a project-by-project approach. They can be designed as instruments that support or deliver planned national development goals, albeit with a lower emission profile than originally planned. Most often they will take the identity of a policy or a piece of regulation, possibly supported by a financing facility or programme, a budget allocation, an incentives scheme or a tax regime, hence being fundamentally indistinguishable from other policy development or regulatory processes. Such an initiative obviously must follow national tradition, in conception, in development, in implementation and in monitoring. The absence of a regulatory environment for the NAMA, therefore, is not the result of negligence, nor is it the result of stalled negotiations and fundamental disagreements among negotiators. It is simply the nature of the NAMA being a 'nationally appropriate' initiative. The decisions outlined above taken by successive Conferences of the Parties to the UNFCCC underscore this fundamental premise.

In a way, the NAMA is a return to the original principles of the Framework Convention, which explicitly recognized that:

Policies and measures to protect the climate system against human-induced change should be appropriate for the specific conditions of each

Party and should be integrated with national development programmes, taking into account that economic development is essential for adopting measures to address climate change (UNFCCC 1992).

Further, the Framework Convention obligated all Parties to 'formulate, implement, publish and regularly update national and, where appropriate, regional programmes containing measures to mitigate climate change by addressing anthropogenic emissions by sources' (Article 4.1 (b)).

Although there are no official definitions of NAMAs the 'official' guidance distinguishes NAMAs along two dimensions. One dimension is the distinction between unilateral versus internationally supported NAMAs. This distinction was made during negotiations mainly for political reasons linked to perceptions of the efforts undertaken by developing countries, signalling that many developing countries and economies in transition do undertake investments – e.g., in renewable energy, which does not receive any support from developed countries.

Furthermore, the distinction is perpetuated by the NAMA Registry,[2] which was established by the UNFCCC Secretariat in 2013, although the unilateral NAMA is called 'other NAMAs, for recognition' in addition to 'NAMAs seeking support for implementation'. The dynamics of NAMA implementation, however, may ultimately render the distinction difficult. Many policy NAMAs can establish business opportunities for the private sector, with investments undertaken by foreign and domestic investors. In the current discourse on the future composition of climate finance, which will be addressed in following chapters, this would challenge what could otherwise be a straightforward definition of unilateral versus internationally supported NAMAs. The phrasing of 'supported NAMAs' may also have connotations for the approach to financing – a distinctly defined activity with a clear start and end, and a financing gap to be closed by a donor – that ultimately could be in conflict with the nature of (many) NAMAs.

Ultimately, most mitigation actions result from investments undertaken in physical assets by any given entity. The NAMA is either the instrument that is employed to bring about such investment by introducing a set of laws and regulations, promotional schemes and possibly an enforcement structure – or it is the investment itself. It is not both, however. This is ultimately a concern for the NAMA host, particularly if he expects financiers or government supported donors to engage on the basis of the prospects for emissions reduction. In that regard, obviously, the same reduction cannot be 'sold' twice.

The other dimension thus is a distinction between 'Policy NAMAs' and 'Project NAMAs'. Some guidebooks and publications, in accordance with many carbon market participants' suggestions, propose a third category, a 'credited NAMA', although this is not supported by negotiation texts. Should a crediting option indeed materialize, i.e., an option to produce Certified Emissions Reductions from NAMAs and export these in a CDM-like fashion, it would still be crediting related to either projects or policies. Only the particular financing model and especially the national accounting for the emissions reduction would be details to consider. A separate category would therefore be redundant.

The 'official' guidance defines Policy NAMAs as actions at the policy/ regulatory level. They require no further intervention by the regulator as they are designed to promote or impose a change of behaviour among the regulated parties, mostly through economic incentives (or disincentives) and change of standards. They are government led (temporary) programmes or measures embodied in (permanent) legislation and implemented through policy instruments. Examples include feed-in tariffs (FiT) for grid-connected renewable energy and building codes setting standards for energy efficiency.

Project NAMAs are specific investments, generally in cleaner infrastructure or machinery. As opposed to the bottom-up approach employed in CDM a project NAMA are more likely to be the result of a political decision and thus result from a more a top-down decision process in which a NAMA host country formulates an appropriate mitigation action, for instance a government decision to construct a 250 MW hydropower plant on a Build Operate Transfer (BOT) basis on a 30 year contract for tendering. It does not stipulate any further hydropower development, nor the conditions for such development should further plants be considered. The difference from the CDM is that the power plant does not generate carbon off-sets for an international carbon market. It could, however, produce carbon off-sets for a national carbon market. In the absence of an international carbon market – *de facto* rather than politically – separate national carbon markets with national jurisdictions are being established, requiring the setting of a general national – or national sector specific – emission cap. Such a cap could constitute a policy NAMA, which if announced as such would prevent a pursuant hydropower project from being listed as a project NAMA in the interest of avoiding double counting.

For a concept with such a limited regulatory foundation this kind of rigidity may be difficult to accept, even though the 'official' NAMA guide states that 'the policy NAMA may be the preferred 'upstream' choice in many cases due to the potential transformational qualities related to policy changes. However, once a NAMA has been devised at the policy level, the resulting 'downstream' actions at the project level should not be recorded as NAMAs again', in accordance with the logic that reductions achieved are not to be double counted. In truth, the

Transforming a sector by changing one word

Many countries have renewable energy policies in place, for a multitude of reasons, including that of emissions reduction. China, for instance, instated a regulation of the national utilities so that for every 100 MW of installed power generation capacity, 2 MW of wind power generation capacity had to be established. This created a rather large niche for domestically produced low cost wind turbines, allowing the installation of their utilities to be regarded as a small tax on coal power without calling for any concern as to the performance of the turbines. Occasionally they were not even connected to the grid.

Obviously, this constituted an unacceptable waste of investment resources, driving the domestic turbine industry in the wrong direction and wasting the opportunity to combat air pollution *and* reduce emissions. By changing the regulation from demanding *generation capacity* requirements to necessitating 2 per cent power generation, the incentives structure for the power utilities was changed completely. It suddenly became important to optimize the power production from the wind turbines. The requirement has since been further increased.

NAMA will either be based on unilateral initiatives by the NAMA host country without the involvement of any official 'NAMA finance' assistance, or on bilateral or multilateral agreements, possibly through the Green Climate Fund once operational, between a NAMA host country and a developed country 'NAMA financier'. Such agreements are currently without any standardization of form and content.

It may be argued that policy and project NAMAs are not covering all options and that short-term programmes are falling through the cracks. The 'official' NAMA guide suggests 'to retire all inefficient coal fired boilers over a period of 24 months or take all sub-standard trucks off the city streets.' Such initiatives, however, will still have to be based on the issuance of regulation to facilitate enforcement – in some cases city or regionally founded regulation as opposed to national level regulation – thus falling in the policy NAMA category.

A conflict in the nature particularly of project NAMAs lies in the growing expectation of transformation. Being identified a fundamental selection criterion for one of the first declared NAMA financiers, the British-German initiated NAMA Facility, the transformational character of a NAMA is expected to become an essential quality sought after by public sector funded NAMA financiers.

Just as NAMAs lack an official definition so is 'transformation' equally without any specific interpretation. The 'official' guidance suggests that the NAMA 'promises transformational change through policy initiatives', but it does not attempt to define what it takes to transform a sector. The text box may inspire a definition, moving from static objectives to operational objectives – in the text box case by changing the performance criterion towards permanent operations. Chapter 7 further discusses transformational NAMAs from a financing point of view.

It is worth noting that the 'official' guidance on NAMAs states that 'NAMAs will often be driven by other priorities than emissions reduction', hence departing from the often artificial reasoning behind CDM projects in order to comply with the additionality principle. NAMAs are not subject to any additionality proof and are only intended to represent a deviation from baseline emissions, seeing emissions reduction as the co-benefit – one that justifies the activation of NAMA finance. The transformation, however, goes beyond emissions. It is a transformation of the way in which a sector generally works in order to meet objectives that are commonly not related to emissions (see textbox).

PoAs and NAMAs

It has been a common perception that the Programmes of Activities (PoAs) under the CDM are a kind of precursors to NAMAs, although a relationship has never been substantiated and a thorough analysis is required.

From the outset the project approach adopted by the CDM was considered a hindrance for larger scale, sector-wide initiatives and rendered also a number of micro-scale actions beyond reach. The Programmes of Activity (PoA) was the response launched in 2005. The PoAs are frameworks that typically cover a sector, e.g., rolling out a particular technology on a larger scale, allowing for successive implementation of activities that are 'included' under the PoA through CDM Programme Activities (CPAs) over time. It is their sector approach that has PoAs often mentioned as precursors to the NAMA.

There are profound challenges in the co-existence of the two. Despite intentions to the contrary, the development of PoAs has become expensive, potentially up to double that of traditional CDM projects. The extra cost is justified by the prospects of including additional CPAs. Therefore, in effect the PoA developer assumes the right to an unquantified 'emissions reduction resource' possibly in competition with other PoA developers that may have established similar PoAs hoping to build up their activity, and business, through inclusion of as many CPAs as possible. While these private sector competitors ideally compete on a level playing field the entry of the government in the establishing of a NAMA in the same sector will be a disturbing factor – particularly if the public sector establishes a supported NAMA with financial contribution from a donor who expects an emissions reduction effect from the investment. Obviously, the same emissions reduction cannot be claimed by the PoA developer and exported out of the country, as that would constitute double counting. Of course, the two can be separated by rigorous measurement, reporting and verification (MRV) protocols – although the advantage of both PoAs and NAMAs should be the exact opposite, namely less stringent MRV, e.g., on the basis of sampling – but that cannot compensate for the loss of business opportunity for the private sector PoA developer.

A solution to the potential conflict could be that the NAMA host government offers to buy the CERs from the PoA on the basis of the financing obtained through the bilateral donor agreement. In that way the private sector remains the prime investor, and the NAMA host government only delivers cash flow. Based on the above there is another area of potential conflict between the two concepts. Assuming that the amount of bilateral financing for the sector intervention is the same – i.e., that the payment for CERs from the PoA is X and the grant for the NAMA is also X – then the payment for the CER, and thus also the export of CERs, must be deducted from the PoA host country's national emission account once the reduction has taken place. Support for the NAMA to the host country does *not* have to have any consequences for the national emission account. In this context the PoA would be more attractive to the donor than the NAMA because the CERs delivered against the contract have a value.

No matter the outcome of any such consideration it points to a judicial intermezzo between the PoA developer, the NAMA host and possibly the NAMA financier. The NAMA should, in fact, be seen as a relief. Projects that have very worthy purposes are being developed as PoAs – for example access to modern energy sources, reading light for school children or improved efficiency of cook stoves often in rural households in the least developed countries. However, the necessity of going through the carbon market, and entertaining the costs affiliated with doing so, to raise capital for these activities, was not questioned. Millions of dollars in donor funds have gone into building capacity for bringing such activities into the carbon market, when the question rather should have been what would be the most efficient way to provide such essentials to these new prospective beneficiaries of the carbon market. The NAMA by and large avoids this detour.

Defining Appropriateness

Since the Convention was drafted in 1992, the enhanced understanding of the urgency to address climate change and the experiences with the Kyoto Protocol has led to negotiations focusing increasingly on engaging all countries in the global mitigation effort while reflecting the Convention principle of Common but Differentiated Responsibilities (CBDR). The Low Emission Development Strategies (LEDS) were introduced in 2010 by the COP in Cancun as a concept that still respected CBDR though doing so in a less explicit manner:

> All countries shall prepare Low Emission Development Strategies … nationally-driven and represent[ing] the aims and objectives of individual Parties in accordance with national circumstances and capacities (Cancun Agreement).

LEDS, in this way, have become an overarching framework to design and achieve Nationally Appropriate Mitigation Actions reflecting the CBDR among countries. In most countries and in many economic sectors concerns about greenhouse gas emissions are finding their way into planning processes and concrete political initiatives. But while many environmental concerns have been mainstreamed in national development planning over the last decades, climate change has yet to be considered a development priority in most developing countries. This may be changing as the consequences of a changing climate are being felt on the ground. It is, for instance, becoming a crucial parameter in China. The most urgent actions focus on damage control – safety measures like dikes against more severe weather, 'designer crops' to withstand more extreme climatic conditions, as well as dedicated mitigation initiatives.

Most initiatives do not stand out as being particularly strategic and few are the result of the low emission development strategies promoted by the negotiation texts. Nevertheless, the Global Environment Facility has responded consciously to its original mandate through a programme of Technology Needs Assessment[3] (TNA) in a number of countries, which were (and still are) to be followed up by technology action plans. However, the limited scope and the severe delay of this activity has seen the TNAs being overtaken by day-to-day policy making, donors' and host countries' eagerness to see action on the ground, and the emergence of new concepts like LEDS and NAMAs. Climate change initiatives, mitigation and adaptation initiatives alike, are, therefore, rarely the product of strategic processes and careful prioritization and planning. Often they are the result of the work of enthusiastic individuals in ministries, NGOs and donors, and at times are brought about in business, as with CDM projects. Such initiatives are not necessarily the most efficient or appropriate mitigation or adaptation responses – but likely the most immediately attractive for the policymaker or the individual project developer, often driven by short-term perspectives.

Appropriateness, fundamentally, is in the eye of the beholder. 'No one can compel me to be happy in accordance with his conception of the welfare of others, for each may seek his happiness in whatever way he sees fit,' to use a Kantian quote.[4] But this naturally works both ways. That means that each nation is free to define national appropriateness in whichever way it sees fit – and each observing nation is free to judge on that expression of appropriateness, applying its own yardstick. If a NAMA is developed for recognition only and does not require developed country finance, the host country does not need to bother with the opinion of others on the appropriateness of their proposed actions – doing so at the risk of attracting only little recognition. However, if a NAMA host is seeking international support, it is unlikely that financing will flow towards mitigation initiatives that a host country finds most befitting, while the donor community disagrees. Therefore, in most cases national appropriateness becomes an issue of mutual concern.

Obviously, these considerations ultimately rest on transparency, but NAMAs may also eventually become the object of unofficial third party 'appropriateness evaluation', just as the Gold Standard Foundation took upon itself to establish its own evaluation criteria for particularly sustainable CDM projects. The CDM faced many concerns when it came into existence – more so than have NAMAs, it appears. One of the main concerns raised was the mechanism's prospective amplification of already existing financial flows bypassing the least developed countries. Various stakeholders had different ideas about what the mechanism ought to support and what should be seen as sub-standard reduction activities. However, since the mechanism was designed as a compliance mechanism delivering off-sets for developed country emitters under restrictions to deliver formally approved off-sets for their excess emissions, it was notoriously difficult to establish a price differentiation on the allowance to emit one tonne of CO_2. A tonne is a tonne, no matter how appropriate or inappropriate spectators may find its source of generation. This was what the Gold Standard Foundation tried to change by establishing a set of additional evaluation criteria.[5]

Developing a similar Gold Standard for the NAMAs would be a daring venture. Appropriateness was not an eligibility criterion for CDM projects, and a free classification of projects did not have any substantial influence on projects and credits that were traded for purposes of compliance with emissions reduction requirements. However, appropriateness is central for NAMAs. Passing judgement on appropriateness for NAMAs may have far reaching consequences and, therefore, will be avoided – at least officially. Just as compliance with sustainability criteria under the CDM was left to the designated national authorities of the host countries, so the determination of the appropriateness of NAMAs will be left to host countries. However, while

Figure 1. NAMAs in the context of general development planning

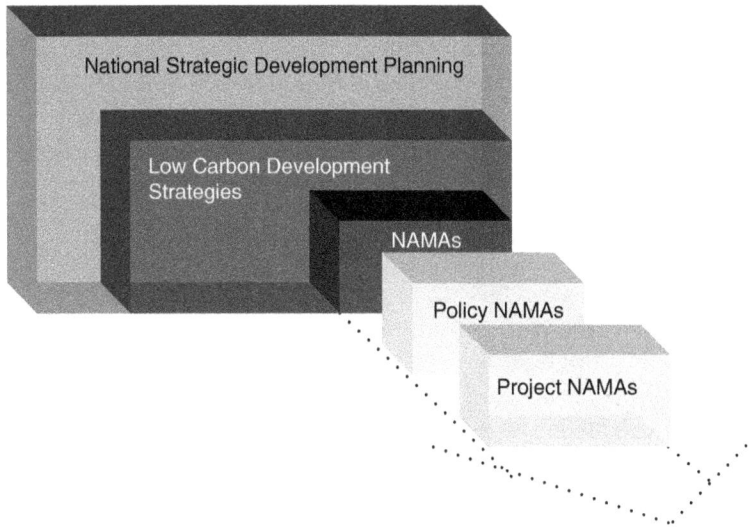

the trustworthiness of this 'sustainability compliance certificate' in the form of a national approval letter for a CDM project was of no consequence for the fundamental performance of the CDM project, in terms of producing emissions allowances, the appropriateness of the NAMA will be put to the test of the financiers. Anyone who ventures to establish a creditable rating system for NAMAs is at a significant risk of calling upon themselves the antagonism of prospective NAMA host countries that see donor funds bypassing due to less favourable ratings. A NAMA rating system would, nevertheless, be welcomed by many stakeholders without their own capacity to assess the credibility of a NAMA host's claims.

In an attempt to define national appropriateness, UNEP Risø's Primer on Low Carbon Development Strategies (UNEP Risø, 2011) uses the graphic presentation in Figure 1 to illustrate the perceived linkages between National Development Plans, Low Carbon Development Strategies (LCDS) and NAMAs. Development planning is a natural activity of any country, regardless of current level of development. Such development planning is aspirational in the sense that it identifies objectives that are believed to be within reach under national circumstances, either through domestic means and initiatives or through the incorporation of development assistance from bilateral and multilateral donors. This sort of development planning, by nature, will identify means and ends that are nationally appropriate, given the national circumstances. The Primer stresses that 'while the LCDS provides the long-term direction – the low carbon development pathway – for the national economy in meeting development goals and objectives, the NAMAs are vehicles to implement the strategy.' While emissions reduction is rarely a separate activity, but rather an option that is linked with an economic activity, and as most countries will likely not be in possession of a Low Carbon Development Strategy, appropriateness is addressed indirectly by the overall development planning. The national appropriateness flows directly from here.

The Substance of NAMAs

Most would intuitively understand the nature of a project NAMA: the project NAMAs have been addressed through the CDM, and prior to that were simply renewable energy projects, energy efficiency projects, waste handling projects or other resource saving initiatives, the implicit effect of which was the reduction of greenhouse gas emissions. As the policy NAMAs are new, the question becomes, what kind of policies could qualify as a policy NAMA?

There seems to be a consensus, at least among donors, that NAMAs must be 'transformational'. While there may be a consensus on the requirement for transformational changes, there is no clear understanding of what it really means. The UK-German NAMA Facility calls itself 'a programme in support of transformational mitigation actions'[6] and states that, 'transformational NAMAs are projects, policies or sector programmes that shift a technology or sector in a country onto a sustainable low-carbon development trajectory.' While this is relatively easy to understand, grasping the true meaning is not straightforward. When can a sector be said to have been transformed? How to ensure a durable transformation? The American and European industries have been transformed during the past two decades by outsourcing their energy intensive production. Surely this is not the kind of transformation that is sought?

Most sectors can be characterized by the way in which financing is flowing within it. The economic actors and the economic systems they operate characterize the state of affairs, the drivers of particular priorities and the outputs in the form of products, services and externalities. It is formed in a balance between the regulator and the regulated. Emissions are an externality, a by-product of an (industrial) activity. Unless regulated against, there is no particular driver for its limitation, except if it clearly has an adverse affect on third parties, which would eventually incur a cost. Such 'self-regulation' is rarely enough for public appeasement. If emissions are to be curbed, it will require an alteration of the economic and financial drivers in a sector – changing the state of affairs, the drivers of particular priorities and the outputs in the form of products, services and externalities. Ultimately,

Table 1. Types of Policy NAMAs (UNEP Risø, 2011)

Policy NAMAs that *represent* action	Policy NAMAs that *require* action
Grants	Energy efficiency target
Direct payment	GHG emission target
Fixed payment	Renewable energy target
Additional payment (e.g. feed-in tariffs)	Other quantitative targets/obligations
Public procurement guidelines	GHG emission below BAU level
Tax credit	GHG mitigation target
Tax reduction/exemption	R&D
Variable or accelerated depreciations	Enhancing forest carbon sinks
Building sector standards	Quota obligations
Labelling requirements for low GHG products	
Removing subsidies	
Loan schemes	
Guarantee schemes	

in the case of climate change policies, 'transformation' is about permanently eliminating or reducing the GHG emission externality of operations in a given sector, while sharing the cost of doing it. Chapter 7 will show how closely linked the financial engineering is to the idea of transformational changes.

Table 1 gives an overview of, and differentiates between, policy NAMAs that are actual steps towards reducing emissions, and those that are too vague to be useful drivers of any reduction of emissions and therefore likely too vague to be called NAMAs (right column). However, developing countries submitted close to one hundred emissions reduction pledges under the Copenhagen Accord in the beginning of 2010, most of which were conditional and for the most part quite diffuse, under the NAMA heading. The 'official guidance' on NAMAs therefore has had to find a way in the middle, choosing not to address these general NAMAs referring to the fact that they are too insubstantial to be the subject of any guidance.

Looking at the options listed in the left hand column, it becomes obvious that most policy NAMAs are initiatives of a financial nature (dark marking). There are low or no emission alternatives to most aspects of societal development – however, they are commonly the more expensive alternative and therefore not chosen. Shifting the priority requires some form of economic incentive – or hard

Figure 2. Weight of policy versus project NAMAs relative to capabilities of developing countries

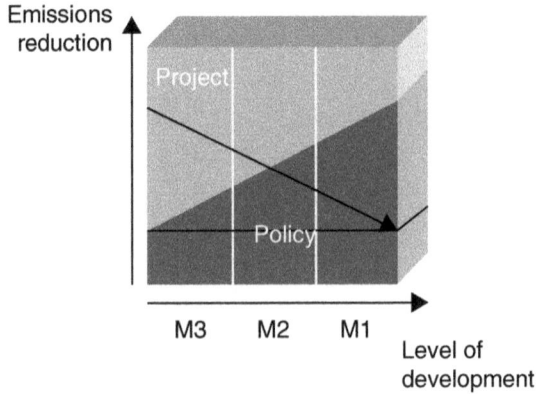

regulation. Soft regulation involving voluntarism and general awareness is clearly not yielding results.

If policy NAMAs are, first and foremost, regulatory and economic in nature, there may be some consequences for their host, in terms of simple capacity considerations. UNEP Risø has introduced a principle, albeit from a capacities perspective for undertaking measurement, reporting and verification routines, wherein countries will (have to) choose between policy and project NAMAs, according to their level of development. In a continuum of development levels, three groups of countries, M1, M2 and M3, are defined. 'Advanced NAMA programmes and policies that tap into elaborate environmental legislation or well-established and efficient energy sector regulation will be most appropriate for countries in group M1, while countries in group M3 may benefit from more project-based approaches that do not rely as much on well-functioning macro systems' (UNEP Risø, 2012).

Figure 2 illustrates the probable weight of activities divided between policy NAMAs and specific project NAMAs as a function of the national capacity to administer MRV systems – a reference which could just as well indicate capacities to administer policy frameworks and regulatory systems that govern activities through a reliable economic incentives system. To the left in the figure are M3 countries that adopt a project-based approach with fewer strategic elements and a more immediate focus on project implementation – much like the CDM approach, which brings its own accounting system for emissions reduction within a defined boundary. 'In these countries policy options are relatively few and enforcement structures relatively weak. Instead, they might concentrate on activities which have obvious parallels to the CDM Programme

Layered, phased and parallel NAMAs

Engineering the financing for a NAMA is not an isolated effort for a single activity, sometimes not even for a single policy. A phasing-out programme for inefficient coal-fired power plants can be paralleled by a nationwide energy efficiency programme that prevents the need to invest in replacement capacity. Saved operational costs for power generation from one NAMA could be directed towards a grant programme for CFLs in another NAMA, and a third NAMA could, e.g., introduce compulsory exchange of inefficient equipment in industry.

One of the first projects supported by the NAMA Facility is a Colombian proposal that combines city planning with transportation, having the two policies supporting each other. Such mutually supporting NAMAs can be very efficient emissions reduction responses, but to the extent that they depend on cross-subsidization as part of the financial engineering they stand and fall together. Ideally, therefore, mutually supporting NAMAs should also be able to serve as standalone activities.

A phased NAMA could introduce a building code for the public sector as a first phase and pursuant phases being targeted at commercial, industry and housing sectors. A parallel NAMA could target efficiency measures in existing buildings, either in general or directed at specific technologies.

A layered NAMA could introduce two or more avenues of emissions reduction in the cement industry, imposing waste heat recovery systems as step 1 (as has been done in China) and incentivizing clinker replacements through the building code mentioned above as step 2.

of Activity or standalone CDM projects. ... In general, the project approach might be more appropriate in countries with less administrative capacity' (UNEP Risø, 2012).

On the right hand side in Figure 2 are countries with well-developed administrative systems that can focus more on policies and regulatory instruments to guide economic sectors towards lower emissions investments. Some of these economies may not require additional external financing for the implementation of policy NAMAs, but they could still benefit from financing instruments that may be developed on account of the climate change agenda. More importantly, they may benefit from mainstream investments of developed country institutional investors if the investment opportunities are sufficiently attractive.

The financing of NAMAs will integrate with already existing political and administrative systems in NAMA host countries and be subject to already existing capabilities, including financing capabilities. NAMAs are not separate activities that require separate financing. To be transformational they must be an integrated part of development and thus integrated parts of the overall financing structure of any given economic sector. There is no magic formula that will eliminate the additional cost that is affiliated with some – but certainly not all – activities, which can or should be considered prospective NAMAs. However, if they are drafted skilfully they may split, rephrase, reschedule or to some extent reduce the cost of emissions reduction.

Summing Up

NAMAs are in many ways the answer to emissions reduction in developing countries, but they are not without challenges – some of which are the same as those that the CDM had to address, particularly the definition of a baseline, but some are simply caused by the legacy of the CDM, which has some market participants promoting that NAMAs should generate tradable emissions reduction units. So far, they may only do so under national cap-and-trade schemes in NAMA host countries. NAMAs are either policies, including regulation and programmes, or they are projects; the latter more relevant for less developed countries with limited administrative capacity. The greatest challenge, however, is that the NAMA is being thought of as a mechanism – which it is not. The NAMA is much more integrated with its host countries' policy framework and development. It thrives predominantly on the regulatory instruments that NAMA host governments have at their disposal, most of which are of a financial character, and requires a much more tangible contribution from the NAMA host, in terms of policy formulation, regulatory enforcement and financing, in order to have NAMAs flourishing with a healthy involvement of donors and the national and international private sectors.

Chapter 3

LEARNING FROM THE CDM

The CDM is indisputably the most successful brand name emerging from the climate change agenda – the flagship of the Kyoto Protocol. Although the previous chapter underlined the difference between NAMAs and the CDM, the two ultimately aim at the same goal: the investment in lower emission alternatives. The CDM has produced a wealth of experience and brought about a much more thorough understanding of what works and what does not when considering the scope and design of NAMAs. First and foremost, the CDM has produced a truly global awareness of the climate change problem and the kinds of actions needed to meet the challenge. The goal of the NAMA is to now bring it to the next level.

The first commitment period of the Kyoto Protocol has ended, and while an extension of the Kyoto architecture was agreed upon at COP18 in Doha, the global climate regime, as we know it, is changing. The CDM is losing its clout and 'new market mechanisms' are urgently sought after. However, before rushing into new approaches to market definition, it is important to look back on the fading CDM, and consider whether its time has come to an end. What would be a reasonable level of activity under the mechanism? Why does the old approach no longer work?

There are many reasons the current carbon market has not worked according to expectation, but that speaks more to the expectations and the ability of policymakers to design a mechanism that responds to real, and in the case of CDMs very complex, market drivers and less to the functioning of the market. With the exception of the American emissions trading program for sulphur dioxide emissions, initiated with The U.S. Clean Air Act Amendments of 1990, there are very few examples of markets trading in externalities. Moreover, the sulphur market is narrow in scope and geography, and benefits from existing in a single judicial system. In the CDM the immense complexities arising from pooling all types of activities and all possible investment drivers, investment climates and national judicial systems into one all-encompassing global market were little understood at the outset – and 10 years later arguably remain little understood.

The most important error in the theory underpinning the CDM is the assumption that all stakeholders have a common objective in reducing the cost of emissions reduction. It is so entrenched in the conceptualization of the CDM that profitable projects that reduce emissions are either 'no regrets' projects or have 'negative costs' – all while investors in these projects regard the ventures as profitable and worthwhile. The Marginal Abatement Cost (MAC) curves have obtained international fame and constitute the foundation for many countries' low carbon development strategies, while the concept of the Marginal Abatement Revenue (MAR) introduced by Lütken and Michaelowa in 2008 has received little attention. Nevertheless, it is an indisputable fact that most, if not all, CDM projects have been undertaken from a profitability perspective, including the profits earned from the carbon market, by project developers and investors that face no cost of emissions reduction – because they exist and operate in developing countries that, in terms of greenhouse gas emissions, remain unconstrained.

The CDM Experience

The CDM was established as a bottom-up, learn-as-you-go mechanism, and for good reason. Never in history had a similar mechanism been devised – one that would generate an entirely new trading unit, which in international transactions would help national governments in meeting their emissions reduction targets. This would be done either through direct purchase or by allowing national corporations to fulfil part of their reduction requirements by surrendering these trading units to their government. It had to be invented from scratch. Even with the Marrakech Accords agreed upon in 2001, which ultimately made the CDM (and the parallel Joint Implementation mechanism) operational, there were still many blanks to fill in – one of the most important being how to calculate the emissions reduction from a given activity and to ensure that this was done consistently throughout the entire prospective pool of similar projects.

This was done by having proponents first file a proposal for a calculation methodology, and only upon its approval submitting their project for another project specific approval. Cumbersome at the outset, and subject to hundreds of revisions, the approach has established a comprehensive library of calculation methodologies, including every possible set of conditions for almost any type of emissions reduction activity – and yet methodologies keep emerging. This will be one of the outstanding legacies of the CDM, and a toolbox, which is unlikely to materialize from any other context. It is a toolbox of lasting value, which can be used as a platform for NAMAs, as well as for the growing number of national emission trading systems that are gradually evolving. Incorporating the CDM methodologies in national trading systems will also facilitate a future linking of such trading systems.

In addition to the methodological toolbox, the CDM has also produced valuable experiences and lessons. For years it has been a mission to upscale the CDM, improve its efficiency and promote its reach into (very cost efficient) sectors not yet covered and countries previously 'underrepresented' in the CDM. There has been little reflection on why such non-market-based intervention should be necessary in a mechanism designed to thrive on market terms. Clearly, either the market operates in unwanted ways, or the mechanism does not reflect the market drivers. When formulating new expectations for NAMAs, these experiences must be taken into consideration. The following is an account of some of these experiences. The imbalances in the CDM are not difficult to understand; if anything, they may be difficult to accept.

The methodological toolbox is not a rose without thorns. The safeguards for the environmental integrity of the mechanism that the toolbox represents has become a burden, the weight of which many worthy projects cannot carry – at least not without the involvement of significant amounts of donor funding. The price of environmental integrity is paid to the advisers and entities established to produce evidence, not only for the activity's adherence to the additionality criterion, but also in the minutest detail for the sources of reduction, the boundaries of the activity, possible leakages outside this boundary and baseline calculations. The result is that for many small-scale projects, the market value of the carbon credits they generate is less than the cost of creating them. Hiding the costs under a donor grant and preventing them from being included in the official profitability calculations that determine the additionality of the activity, are circumventions that resemble practices in less liberal economic systems.

Part of the misfortune is the carbon price, which results from a supply and demand equilibrium, and which again is a consequence of many other factors. The CDM's vulnerability to market forces, as demonstrated in 2012, may be a serious deterrent to future project development driven by a carbon market, unless mechanisms that can counterbalance price extremes are added. It may well be that future calls for private sector investments on the basis of any mechanism or concept devised by the international climate negotiations, including the NAMA, will be met with suspicion and distrust. That would be regrettable, as the NAMA not only cuts through the rigid methodological platform upon which the CDM is based, but also accepts that projects are undertaken for other purposes than merely emissions reduction. Therefore, the mitigation actions need neither demonstrate additionality, nor claim to be a result of a concern for the climate.

It's a market – live with it

The immense surplus supply of CERs by mid 2012 contributed to a collapse of international carbon prices. The CER lost its pegging to the 'EU Allowance' (EUA) in the European Emission Trading System (EU ETS),[1] and fell from a high of more than EUR 15 in the EU ETS in 2009 to below EUR 1 in 2012. While some would claim that this was a failure of the carbon market, others would maintain that the market does not fail – it simply reflects the indisputable fact that more CERs are produced than the market demands. This results from flaws in the design of the carbon market on *both* sides. Had investors been prudent on the supply side, the current flooding of the markets would not have happened. Had regulators been vigilant on the demand side, mechanisms would have been put in place to clearly prevent market access as a deterrent to investments or design absorption mechanisms if, indeed, it was thought that the CERs deserved a better fate. The European Commission did try to delay the auctioning of 900 million allowances for several months (years), but it proved to be too little too late.[2]

Prudence on the supply side requires a sufficient amount of attention to the business, and this is where the disconnect between the carbon market and the underlying asset rests. Despite the attempt to elevate the emissions externality to an investment driver, it has remained an externality. With a price on carbon, the externality, however, has been a positive one, in the sense that the emissions reduction by-product was attributed a value, which, once exploited, spurred the development of a new cadre of consultants specializing in the capitalization of this by-product. It never managed to really influence the core activities that were unrelated to the demand for credits. Subsequently, the consultants kept capitalizing the by-product of these activities far beyond demand – mainly because the only cost of doing so was that of the documentation, and not the cost of the asset. The positive consequence of these somewhat skewed market drivers is that the market collapse has not left thousands of developing country investors with stranded assets; the main casualty is the consulting businesses with obsolete capacities for producing CDM documentation. There is one exception: owners of CDM projects with only one source of income through the carbon credits, who have not secured their carbon assets through forward emissions reduction purchase agreements. They are indeed casualties of a collapsing carbon market; these 'one-revenue stream' projects constitute about 4 per cent of the entire portfolio of registered CDM projects.[3]

Market volatility and market intervention are two essential factors that developing country policy makers should consider in relation to potential inclusion of a national carbon market as an instrument for promoting emissions reduction through NAMAs. This is particularly the case if plans include an international link as has been seen in Japan's bilateral offset crediting mechanism. In national trading schemes, should they emerge as a result of NAMAs, national control of supply and demand can contain the worst market extremes and provide the stability that investors are ultimately looking for.

Thriving on domestic finance

When the CDM was elaborated from a concept at COP3 in Kyoto to operationalization at COP7 in Marrakech, one of the main concerns among potential project host countries was investor certainty and project risks.[4] The CDM, being a market-based mechanism, carried the inherent risk that it would leave the unattractive investment climates unattended. When finally agreed upon, the CDM provided access to exploiting least-cost reduction options in developing countries. However, the CDM was an option, not an obligation. The expectation was that investor capital originating from developed countries in search of cost efficient emissions reduction options would be diverted towards developing countries' energy, transport and agriculture sectors – if conditions were right. They hadn't been earlier. They still weren't.

If the 'where-flexibility' did not provide sufficiently attractive emissions reduction investment options in developing countries, it was to be expected that investments would concentrate on emissions reduction compliance activities in developed countries. However, that was not the case either. It turned out, surprisingly, that developing country investors were ready to put up the investment capital that their emission constrained peers in developed countries were not. There were indications early on (e.g., Lütken and Michaelowa, 2008) that projects materializing under the CDM were not results of foreign investments in low cost reduction options. In 2012, the UNFCCC Secretariat acknowledged that possibly as much as 95 per cent of investment capital in CDM projects originated from developing countries (Kirkman et al., 2012).

The fact that the CDM has not been able to mobilize any significant investment capital from developed countries, but only cash flow, represents two important realizations:

1) Investments in CDM projects are overwhelmingly in countries that can raise investment capital domestically
2) Attracting investment capital from developed countries into developing countries requires stronger incentives than the CDM in its design has been able to deliver.

The NAMA, being a concept and not a mechanism, does not contain any means to alter these fundamentals. Foreign Direct Investment (FDI) will inevitably be overshadowed by local investment, as it is in nearly all economies. Depending on the interpretation of the transformations that NAMAs are expected to promote, the NAMA may support not only an increasing level of investment in targeted sectors, but may also help establish investment conditions that are both nationally appropriate, and conducive to increased foreign investment. The CDM has shown that increasing the profit from such investments is not sufficient. It has also been shown that NAMA host countries must realize that the prime audience, and foremost investors, of the transformations that they are to promote through NAMAs remain within the local business environment. This, once again, signifies that NAMAs are not equally relevant for all countries. Similar to the initial concern raised for the CDM, they may perpetuate and accentuate current flows of capital and investment, and leave the least developed economies unattended – which would equally be in accordance with the emissions reduction potential.

Small is beautiful ...

Keeping it small does not always make for good business. The distribution of CDM projects was a concern even before the mechanism was finally agreed upon. The concern was that it would only reinforce existing investment patterns rather than altering them. The Nairobi Framework[5] was agreed upon by the COP in 2005 to counter the imbalances recorded. The assessment of an 'unequal access to the carbon market', however, was a rather simplistic one, revealing that smaller countries had less project activities than larger countries, and that least developed countries – many of which were riddled with war or conflict – were seeing less activity than well-functioning countries. Moreover, even in a relative assessment comparing national emissions to emissions reductions achieved through the CDM, least developed countries had fallen behind in 2005 (Lütken, 2011). CDM projects were mainly occurring in the large economies of China, India and Brazil, and a few others – as were investments, in general. The CDM did indeed follow already existing patterns of investment.

There are many reasons for this, the most important one stemming from the above mentioned fact that CDM projects thrive on domestic investment capital that least developed countries cannot raise. Other reasons relate to the challenge of smaller national economies fostering smaller projects. Small energy sectors, low grid emission factors, or a focus on household interventions and micro-scale investments do not match the CDM's core low cost reduction objective – even if the activity in itself is an economically attractive intervention – because the costs of documentation for the CDM are relatively fixed and sometimes even exceed the value of the entire emissions reduction. The Programmes of Activity have sought, but not succeeded decisively, to address this issue, as market forces have driven up prices for the documentation of PoAs[6] and the issuance of CERs from such programmes. Since the conception of PoAs in 2005, the issuance of CERs from PoAs were still fewer than 150,000 by January 2014.[7]

The little that the UNFCCC Secretariat has been able to do in terms of administrative exemptions and the capacity building and awareness raising fostered by the Nairobi Framework may have caused the reduced imbalance measured (Lütken, 2011), although the causality between the capacity building and CDM project development is difficult to establish. Investment fundamentals, however, remain unchanged.

Cost inefficient emissions reduction

Looking at the characteristics of the CDM projects that have been developed so far – more than 12,000 projects are now recorded of which more than 7,000 were officially registered by the end of 2013 – it is becoming clear that their materialization is based on very different investment drivers. This is due to a few missing links that were overlooked in the design of the CDM: it was never established whether developed country investors would go as far as to shift their investment strategies for the sake of emissions reduction; and it was never established with any certainty whether investments with emissions reduction purposes were actually motivated by the lowest cost of emissions reduction.

Figure 3 illustrates the distribution of 'carbon returns' on investment – according to information from the CDM Pipeline[8] about 984 projects distributed on 10 sectors. A 'pre-market-collapse' price of 12 USD/CER is used, reflecting the typical forward contract on price in Emissions Reduction Purchase Agreements (ERPA) in 2006–2008 with an overweight on the high-priced Chinese market, which was controlled by an unofficial floor price regime policed by the Chinese DNA.[9] The calculation shows the value of the annual CER production relative to the investment in the underlying asset. Wind energy and hydropower projects are to the far left in the graph with average annual returns from the carbon market of 1 to 4 per cent of the investment. At the other end of the spectrum are very profitable industrial gasses and manure projects that fall within the small category that have the carbon revenues as their only income stream. About 600 billion USD, by far the largest amount, had been invested in wind and hydro with the expected generation of 650 million CERs by the end of 2012, while only about

Figure 3. Emissions reduction returns on investment in the CDM

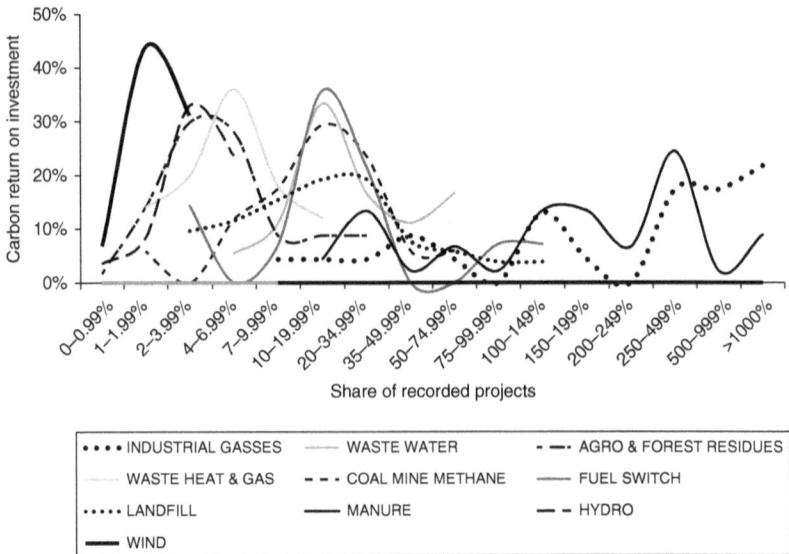

INDUSTRIAL GASSES · · · ·   WASTE WATER ——   AGRO & FOREST RESIDUES – —·

WASTE HEAT & GAS ——   COAL MINE METHANE – – ·   FUEL SWITCH ——

LANDFILL · · · · ·   MANURE ——   HYDRO — –

WIND ——

50 billion was invested in industrial gases and manure projects generating more than 800 million CERs. Thus, most of the capital invested in CDM projects has gone into some of the least cost efficient emissions reduction options.

There are many examples of this also from developed countries as well, particularly on support schemes for solar PV power generation in private households, e.g., in Germany and Denmark. Despite efforts in producing marginal abatement cost curves to inform policy makers of the most efficient way to curb greenhouse gas emissions, the initiatives supported by national policies most often disregard these curves and move ahead with other more expensive alternatives.

It is clear that drivers other than the value of the emissions reduction are at play, indicating that different sectors compete on different platforms, and have widely differing interests in emissions reduction. If it is evident that emissions reduction is only a driver in *some* of the activities that are recorded as reduction activities, it becomes equally clear that the emissions reduction effect of many activities has evolved into a positive externality. For that very reason, the Marginal Abatement Revenue mentioned earlier is a much better reflection of the market drivers. Floating these residuals of other sector strategies may or may not disturb the drivers in the 'real' carbon market that should, but clearly do not, reflect the balancing of supply and demand of cost efficient emissions reduction.

Therefore, identifying the crucial drivers in those specific technology markets and aligning initiatives in the form of NAMAs with these drivers, which seems to be the evolving discourse for NAMA development according to the 'official' NAMA guidance, is evidently the correct course of action. Accordingly, it becomes obvious that cost *in*efficiency of emissions reduction does not make a mitigation action *in*appropriate.

Additionality revisited

As per the Kyoto Protocol, emission reductions resulting from a project activity must provide real, measurable and long-term benefits related to the mitigation of climate change, as well as 'reductions in emissions that are additional to any that would occur in the absence of the certified project activity' (Kyoto Protocol, Article 12(5)). The additionality requirement is the most debated, contested and criticized principle in the CDM since the conception of the mechanism. While the additionality of projects is indispensable for the environmental integrity of the CDM due to the offsetting of emissions elsewhere relative to the crediting, the proof of additionality has – for the lack of better ideas – been by proxy only. Moreover, often it has required information that no investor would be in possession of – for instance the average internal rate of return (IRR) of similar projects in a given sector. Such requirements push project sponsors into circumventions that undermine the very purpose of the exercise. Additionality proof is a construct that the market will have to bypass simply out of necessity, regardless of the true additionality of any given project.

Additionality and baselines are indispensable instruments for the way in which the Kyoto Protocol's flexible mechanisms have had to demonstrate their emissions reduction effect, but neither are particularly workable concepts. There can only be deemed baselines and deemed additionality. Even in clear-cut cases where one inefficient boiler is replaced by a new efficient one, baseline arguments end up considering normal lifetimes and common retirement practices for such a technology. Eventually, they arrive at a choice among a number of possible futures, a number of years of crediting based on the most likely scenario, resulting in a deemed baseline.

Unlike the CDM, NAMAs are free from any additionality requirements. The baselines remain, however, and while they continue to be debatable they are necessary for calculating an approximate emissions reduction effect of a given NAMA. Moreover, it remains disputable which national policies and projects are part of the baseline and which are NAMAs, recalling the perverse incentive discussions raised by the World Bank in the early days of the CDM. These ultimately led to the E+ and E- regulations in the CDM (see textbox), designed to ensure that sensible policies (e.g., promoting or setting national targets for renewable energy) should not disqualify projects for the CDM, even

---

E+ and E- in NAMAs

With baseline assessment as the only instrument to determine the emission reduction effect of NAMAs, E+ and E- as developed for the CDM are bound to become central.

According to the CDM Rulebook (http://cdmrulebook.org/4962), E+ policies are national and/or sectoral policies or regulations that give comparative advantages to *more* emissions-intensive technologies or fuels over less emissions-intensive technologies or fuels, whereas Type E- policies are national and/or sectoral policies or regulations that give comparative advantages to *less* emissions-intensive technologies or fuels over more emissions-intensive technologies or fuels.

Following CDM Executive Board guidance, the impact of Type E+ policies implemented after 11 December 1997 and Type E- policies implemented after 11 November 2001 are not to be taken into account when developing a baseline scenario (EB 22, Annex 3).

Similar exemptions or other forms of guidance are likely to become in demand when NAMA development and finance accelerates.

---

though such CDM projects should be seen as responses to already adopted policies and, thus, considered as part of the baseline.

Reverse engineering the CDM

Effectively, the CDM has been the testing ground for the feasibility of elevating a traditional externality into becoming an investment driver. The idea, at least in the form that has been attempted in the CDM, seems unfeasible. With a few revisions, however, a CDM-like instrument could be a viable instrument in NAMAs.

The CDM has depended on an international market that links differing framework conditions, differing investment drivers and various regulatory requirements, which has become a marketplace for a mix of residuals of other initiatives and policies (positive externalities) and some real reduction initiatives. The NAMAs could be at risk of treading the same path, albeit in a less complex national context, unless the national regulator refrains from devising rigid additionality tests and stays with the requirement for a deviation from the baseline. Even the baseline assessment could be eliminated as long as projects are obvious low emission or emission free investments – or simply actions that are sensible from a number of viewpoints, including the emissions reduction argument.

The World Bank's Partnership for Market Readiness (PMR)[10] is likely the most advanced framework for the development of New Market Mechanisms which are negotiated as part of a new international climate agreement – much in the same way that the World Bank spearheaded the development of CDM projects through the Prototype Carbon Fund before the Marrakech Accords established the regulatory framework. The work has resulted in a number of common themes listing the prime challenges (of which there are many) for countries that consider including trading mechanisms either as domestic instruments or as CDM-like structures with export of off-sets.[11] Questions raised concern how to build in flexibility and updating in rules and how credited reductions sold/used internationally will be accounted for to avoid double counting. The long list of themes revisits many of the fundamentals for CDM and market mechanisms in general, but seems to avoid the main challenge in the CDM.

The CDM's main challenge has been its inability to secure any significant financing motivated and quantified by the relative emissions reduction resulting from the activity. The current ex-post approval of CDM projects and CERs by the UNFCCC Executive Board and the market commonality to pay for CERs only on delivery has led to the popular notion that CERs are only 'the icing on the cake' in an investment calculus. Revenues from CERs are simply made too uncertain to serve as collateral in a financing model by subjecting first the registration of the project and then the issuance of CERs for later approval by the Executive Board. Therefore, future cash flows from CERs cannot be converted into present asset finance.

In effect, the approval system itself has helped marginalize the importance of the cash flow from the carbon market.

The financing potential of the carbon asset can only be achieved if the issuance of CERs could be guaranteed, thereby securing the cash flow, which is at the core of the banks' requirements. The operation of the CDM over the past 10 years could facilitate such guarantees. Over the years, a large statistical basis for project performance, in terms of CER issuance, has been established (as illustrated in Figure 2). For instance, a wind turbine project in India has an average CER issuance rate of 84 per cent, as compared to expectations. Waste heat recovery projects are likely to deliver about 79 per cent of the projected emissions reduction, regardless of geography. About 90 per cent of CDM projects fall under categories for which a reasonable statistical basis has been established for the determination of likely issuance.

While the emissions reduction figures for wind energy and hydropower are unimpressive compared to the required investment, their accumulation over 5 to 10 years could still amount to 10 to 20 per cent or more of the actual

Figure 4. From ex-post to ex-ante approvals in CDM

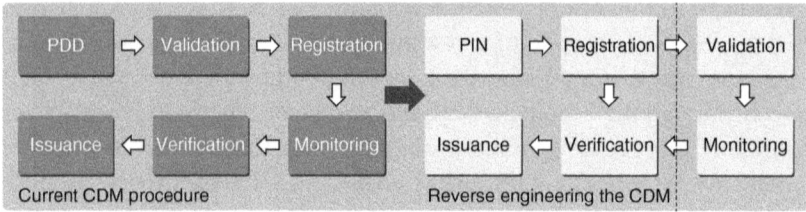

investment, if the carbon prices were intact. This would certainly be valuable if it arrived during the financial engineering of the project. Even in the depressed 2013 CER price regime, 7 years of accumulated CER revenues – e.g., for waste heat recovery projects – could still be a relevant financial package of up to 10 per cent of the investment.

For a number of technologies, the statistical basis can be used in a 'reverse engineering' of the approval process for the CDM. Specifically, an approval process that only needs to involve the UNFCCC Secretariat giving out guarantees for CER issuance, based on the statistical expectation and basic project data – for example, in a PIN (Project Information Note) format. A smaller or larger 'conservativeness premium' could be deducted from the project's expected amount of emissions reduction. The only requirement for the project developer would be that the project must be built – equally required by all other financing stakeholders. Depending on the technology in question, the guarantee should cover a number of years of CER issuances in order to have any substantial financing leverage. A UNFCCC guaranteed issuance of, e.g., 500,000 CERs for 7 years of operation of a waste heat recovery project, combined with an ERPA with a reputable buyer, will stand a much better chance of being accepted as collateral in a local or international bank, than current ERPAs without a UN guarantee. Project developers that wish to have more precise (higher) issuance rates could continue the normal route beyond the dashed line in Figure 4.

This is valid for the international carbon market, which is currently facing much more severe challenges in the form of a significant surplus supply. While the reverse engineering of the CDM will address most problems, it will not create new demand. New national trading schemes incorporating project-based activities, resembling Joint Implementation rather than CDM, will most likely not require UN-based guarantees for credit issuance; national guarantees would suffice. However, with reference to one of the themes identified under PMR, a crediting model without any guarantees involved is unlikely to influence the fundamental investment drivers in any country – and in all probability at any carbon price, as long as markets are without any safety mechanisms to reduce the risk of market collapse. As such markets unavoidably are political constructs without any support of a physical product, such a risk can probably only be fully mitigated by sovereign contracts – or partly mitigated by guarantee institutions (see Chapter 8).

Using CDM-like instruments in national emission reduction strategies is a viable option, but it cannot be based on utopian assumptions of new international demand for off-sets. It can, however, be based on national frameworks and NAMAs that promote emissions reduction through cap-and-trade systems. In a NAMA context, the CER issuance guarantees that the UNFCCC would provide following the above model, would obviously be for a NAMA host country authority to take responsibility for. The target of such national issuance guarantees would predominantly be the domestic industry – the investors activated equally and primarily of national origin. FDI *driven* mitigation is not realistic, but through the NAMA and such domestically guaranteed cash flows there is a chance to plan for its involvement.

Summing Up

The CDM was a great experiment that yielded immense amounts of experience, without which it would be impossible to develop new and efficient approaches for involving developing countries in the emissions reduction agenda. However, it must not be deemed a success simply because it appears to be the most tangible outcome of the Kyoto Protocol. It certainly has its legacies – and even though it seems to be only a shadow of its former self, it is still alive. It has been documented that result-based financing for private sector investment is not a viable option unless it is supported by guarantees that bolster the financiers' confidence in the actual delivery of results. Without such guarantees, private sector investments would have to thrive on the cash flows that are trusted and can be financed. This is the most important lesson learnt from the CDM, and it should be heeded in any discussion on transformational NAMAs that seriously involve the private sector's financial capacities. Had this been realized from the outset, and had the UNFCCC regulator been bolder in offering certainty following the suggested principles in the reverse engineering of the CDM, most of the controversies in the CDM may well have been avoided.

Chapter 4

DEFINING NAMA FINANCE

> There is not sufficient public capital to finance all that is needed to meet the 2 degree target. The private sector will have to contribute.

While this is not a direct quote, it captures a common perception that the climate challenge cannot be met only by public sector financing initiatives, but must rely on significant contributions from the private sector. The estimates of the amount required from the private sector vary, particularly in relation to the capitalization of the Green Climate Fund (see Chapter 9). UNEP's Finance Initiative suggests that at least 85 per cent must originate from the private sector (UNEP FI, 2012). It could be argued that this is a somewhat artificial separation in the sense that the public sector's funds were also once private. Asking the private sector to contribute is another way of indicating that increasing the share of funds channelled through the public sector by raising taxes is not believed to be a viable option – and might not be efficient either.

Fundamentally, there are four overall categories of financing related to NAMAs. They form a matrix like this:

	Public	Private
Domestic	1	3
Foreign	2	4

A split between public and private finance could suffice, but the division on domestic and foreign sources of finance reflects the international negotiation texts on NAMAs – e.g., FCCC/AWGLCA/2010/8 from the 2010 Cancun Agreement, which differentiates between supported and unilateral NAMAs. The text articulates the requirement for developed countries to make finance, technology and capacity building available for developing countries' implementation of NAMAs.

Once the funds are in the public sectors' hands, they are prioritized and administered for a multitude of public sector purposes in a finance bill.

It is here that allocations to specific climate-related initiatives are made – or not made, due to scarcity of funds, or other less financial reasons.

It is popular to call for 'innovative financing models' as a desirable foundation for NAMAs. Innovative financing models would be ways, as yet undiscovered, in which the two sectors, public and private, interact, but it is unlikely that such innovative capacity would stem from a financial sector that is globally being punished for its overly innovative financing arrangements. If anything, the financial sector would stick to business as it used to be. Instead, innovative capacity is more necessary in public–*public* partnerships. If innovation is needed in the finance sector, it would be interesting to reflect on *why* the climate cause should require such innovation, or why the climate cause should need to exempt itself from fundamental financing principles. Making the financing work for the climate should be about tweaking existing instruments, not creating brand new ones or introducing new and untested principles, which hold significant risks of getting it wrong – similar to the CDM, in many respects. It is not about duplicating existing financing offers, either.

This is not in conflict with the growing expectation that the lion's share of the financing for climate relevant investments will stem from the private sector, including the private banking sector. 'Mobilizing' private capital is the term used to describe this, and 'leveraging' is the sought after mechanics that will ensure that a small move by the public sector would lead to significant movement in private business. Ultimately, in many cases it is private business, supported by the banks, that will invest. A gross simplification would have private capital investment driven only by profitability, or more specifically risk/return considerations, i.e., that a greater risk should be rewarded with a greater return. Sometimes, such simplifications are useful. Risks are barriers that need to be overcome or removed to mobilize the private capital. Certain risks and risk levels are acceptable, while others are not – meaning, not all risks need to be removed entirely, nor can they all be compensated for by a higher return, because the chance of winning does not grow with the size of the prize. Private capital investment is not a lottery. By contrast, it is not always the case that public financing dispositions are driven by cost efficiency. It is even rarer that they would be driven by considerations of profitability.

At this point, a definition of climate finance, or NAMA finance in particular, would be useful. Since the establishment of the Global Environment Facility, the 'incremental cost' approach to climate financing has been a prevailing term used by policymakers to illustrate the financing gap for the emission friendly alternatives. Incremental costs have been defined by the GEF as the difference between costs of a baseline development and costs incurred in a project or policy scenario. In other words, incremental costs are 'additional costs associated with transforming a project with national benefits into one with global environmental benefits' (GEF, 2011),[1] but it is worth asking, 'the incremental cost to whom?' The investor in a wind power plant does not consider any part of the plant as an additional cost; neither does the utility rehabilitating a coal-fired power plant with an efficient boiler or a combined cycle.

The incremental cost could be calculated on the basis of different *versions* of the technology being installed. A waste heat recovery system for a steel plant comes in a low cost version with payback times of 4 years, or a high cost version with double that. Choosing high cost over the low cost option could be an incremental cost, but the decision may well be made on the assumption that the high cost option is the cheaper solution over the lifetime of the plant and, therefore, constitutes a low cost option.

Incremental costs should not be confused with high investment costs, which certainly are a hindrance for many investments in a multitude of high investment cost/low consumption technologies, be it demand side energy consuming equipment, or supply side renewable energy technology. In many cases, however, the high investment cost returns to the investor, in the form of a positive net present value (NPV). If the NPV is negative, it may carry an incremental cost – or may simply be bad business. The typical investors in these technologies do not entertain an incremental cost. They engineer their financing to meet the cost of an investment that is evaluated on its risk-adjusted returns. The incremental cost is entertained outside the investors' investment calculations.

The incremental costs approach is, therefore, much more complex than its immediate appeal. It is certainly the cost that is in focus where the financial engineering of NAMAs is concerned, but it needs to be entertained in other structures, and by entities other than those investing in the more expensive emissions reduction technology. The common choice of wording is that a *country* entertains the incremental cost, which is an imprecise and general statement but perhaps comes closer to the core of the meaning, if referring to the national budget.

The trouble is that in most contexts, 'climate finance' is regarded not only as the incremental cost, but as the *entire* investment. The Climate Policy Initiative's Climate Finance Project (Climate policy Initiative, 2012a) mapped in detail financial flows into activities that beyond their central service (like e.g. energy supply) also provides 'climate service'. CPI estimates that annual global climate finance flows reached an average 364 billion USD in 2010 and 2011, including $217 to 243 billion, or 63 per cent of the total, from the private sector. Public development finance represented 5 to 6 per cent of the overall flow, and was channelled mainly through bilateral aid, of which a growing share is devoted to climate finance and support to the private sector, whereas USD 293 billion was in the form of market rate loans and equity. A third of all mitigation investments happened in NAMA host countries, albeit without being labelled as NAMAs, the bulk of which was spent in emerging economies.

There seems to be an important assumption that the private sector actually provides climate financing. This may be disputed, although mainly from a semantic perspective. The private sector finances profitable projects that happen to have climate change mitigation benefits. The profitability is either inherent in the technology choice or it is resulting from a regulatory environment encompassing one or more of the regulatory instruments listed in Table 1. This may help in defining NAMA finance, which in this context pertains much more to the financing of these regulatory instruments than to the asset financing also addressed by the traditional climate finance definition of which, thus, NAMA finance can be regarded a subset.

In project finance, 'feasible' refers to projects that are technically doable regardless of the economy. 'Viable' projects are feasible projects that under realistic assumptions produce acceptable returns on investment as determined by the investor. A project is only 'bankable', however, if such returns are produced with a sufficient level of certainty as *perceived* by third party financiers, typically banks, who are convinced that the project can service the debt. Therefore, most financial engineering is about comforting the banks.

The same can be said for the financial engineering of NAMAs – even though the NAMA financing chain is longer than that of isolated private project finance. This is not as unfair as it may sound. Banks traditionally provide the largest share of total project financing – which is also the case in climate-related investments – and they do so at the start-up phase, when the risk is the highest and all forecasts are put to the test. Banks depend on future cash flows to repay the loans. If cash does not flow in the expected quantity, the risk of default becomes real. Conversely, if cash flows more readily than expected, there is no upside for the banks – i.e. they only receive an interest on the loan, not a share of the profit. Therefore, they cannot balance losses against profits.[2]

The financial engineering of NAMAs is not about convincing the banks to change their ways. Even if they would, Basel III[3] has ensured the banking sectors' prudence. It is not about discarding the banks either. The banks are the private sector's closest allies. If the private sector's financial involvement in NAMAs is crucial, the financial engineering is about providing conditions that allow the private sector and its banking partners to engage together. Therefore, it can be argued that:

NAMA finance is the financing that must be engineered in order to allow the private sector *and* their banking partners to do their business as usual.

That means investing in profitable business propositions – albeit in this context these investments must have emissions reduction benefits. This definition circumvents lengthy debates about the identity of climate finance. Is it the USD 240 billion invested in renewable energy generation capacity in 2012 (ref. IEA) or is it the estimated USD 13 billion paid for Certified Emissions Reductions (CERs) from the CDM (assuming USD 10/ CER issued), or is it the GEF's USD 3 billion investment in climate related projects? Or is it the USD 364 billion estimated by the Climate Finance Project in 2012?

Some advocate NAMA budgeting on the basis of incremental costs while others adopt a total cost approach, which has already been discarded above. A third more pragmatic approach, which is the one adopted here, would be to structure the national and international finance in a public–public partnership, orchestrating the financing model and financial instruments as efficiently as possible and devising a structure for the lowest cost option that allows the private sector to take care of the remaining finance. These costs may or may not add up to the traditional incremental cost.

The approach has profound consequences for the definition of what is 'inside' and 'outside' the NAMA financing structure. If the private sector is not likely to, and not presumed to, revise its 'for profit' investment motivation, only the public sector will be actively engaged in engineering the NAMA financing. Other financial engineering succeeding in the private sector will not differ from what is already on-going business. The innovative capacity for NAMA financing is therefore to be rooted in public–*public* partnerships (see Figure 5) and less so in public–private partnerships (PPP) – although PPP is a very important model for NAMA *implementation*.

Essentially, however, while the illustration indicates that the financial engineering of the NAMA succeeds in the public-public realm, it does not mean that the instruments devised should not target the private sector actors. On the contrary, most instruments serve the purpose of improving the profitability of private sector investments.

Very few investments are undertaken for the purpose of emissions reduction alone, or even with the emissions reduction objective as the prime driver, as already pointed out by the 'official' NAMA guidance. In that regard, the fundamental question becomes whether an instrument can be devised to serve several parallel purposes. The CDM has had these parallel purposes incorporated though other objectives were treated as not being of equal importance – hence the term co-benefits. But even co-benefits are objects for evaluation, and CDMs flanks

Figure 5. Financial engineering of NAMAs

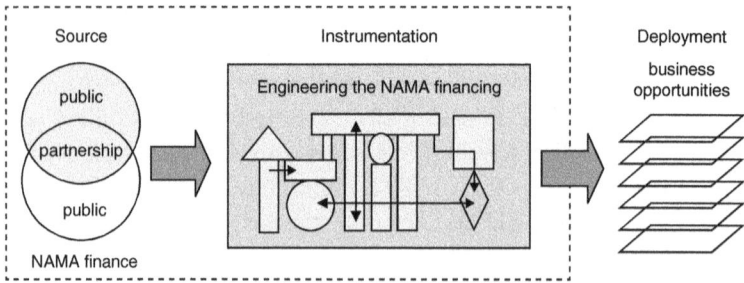

have been open for criticism because different stakeholders have used their own interpretations and definitions, particularly for technology transfer and sustainable development.

The true driver of a given activity can normally be evaluated qualitatively by asking who would invest in this activity – and for what purpose. In that respect, it is of no avail if there are two or more stakeholders willing to invest in the activity for differing reasons. That inherently translates into conflicts of interest. Designing the NAMA entails the identification of the one investment driver around which a financing model is structured. If other stakeholders can see their interests reflected in the activity, that is advantageous, but the design of a NAMA must focus on the single objective that is likely to deliver the bulk of the finance. Hence, in most instances, climate – and NAMA – finance will have to engage in purposes other than emissions reduction.

Government Investment Motives

Governments provide public goods, including emissions reduction, and can pursue many different objectives with one single initiative. In line with the fundamental definition of emissions as an externality to other economic activities, the emissions reduction effect will be the co-benefit related to other prime objectives, such as: reducing congestion, reducing dangers of explosion in landfills, preventing hazardous emissions from old power plants, improving security of supply, providing energy access, substituting imports, reducing subsidies, pursuing targeted industrial development, or a host of other motivations.

By not addressing the (real) motivation behind a given NAMA, there is a risk that the initiative represents a business as usual (BAU) scenario in emission terms. This is fundamentally an issue between the NAMA proponent and the financier of the emission reduction objective. The BAU scenario is essential for the funding motivated by emissions reduction, but not for other sources of finance. These will most often be driven by immediate public good objectives, if it is the public sector providing financing – or by profit motives, as far as private sector financing is concerned.

In the previous chapter, it was established that most investment capital in the CDM has gone into the least cost efficient emissions reduction options in wind and hydropower. Assuming that an IRR contribution of more than 3 per cent per year is required from the carbon market to represent a cost efficient emissions reduction alternative, at least 75 per cent of the investment capital in CDM as a whole has gone into projects that do not represent cost efficient emissions reduction (Lütken, 2012). However, as mentioned above, projects can also be motivated by many other considerations or simply by shifting investments to the private sector.

Cost *in*efficiency, in terms of emissions reduction, does not render projects reckless reduction adventures. If the real benefit is measured on the basis of other parameters, the emissions reduction is a co-benefit where the cost is not necessarily calculated. This does not prevent the activity from being listed as a NAMA – particularly if the project represents a deviation from the original mode of implementation (see Figure 6). Additionally, in emissions reduction terms, a short-term high price may be a necessary cost to drive technology prices down through demand.

Prevention of investment in high cost reduction options through NAMAs is, therefore, not an objective in itself. Cost *in*efficient emissions reductions are fundamentally not an investment deterrent (Lütken, 2012). Nor are the chances to successfully engineer the financing around such a NAMA necessarily influenced by the high costs of abatement. High profile government projects may be good investment objects, although they may also be volatile if their viability is dependent on continuous political support that can be revoked in case of a changing government.

It ultimately comes down to the fact that emissions reduction is only rarely a separate focus. As underscored by the 'official' NAMA guidance, it is a parameter that is taken into consideration along with a number of other development parameters and priorities, which are more important for national development. Other primary concerns drive development in areas of health and education, agriculture and industry development, transportation and energy supply. Many NAMAs, therefore, are adjustments of development, geared at planning to reduce their carbon footprint downwards to a lower level of emissions. This relates to the baseline and the estimation of emissions reduction resulting from a particular NAMA.

Figure 6. Sub-optimal investments in emissions reduction

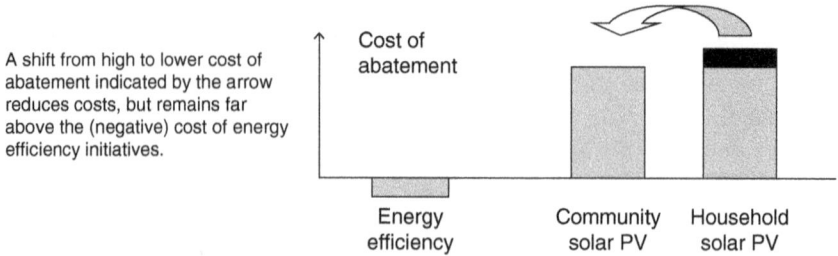

A shift from high to lower cost of abatement indicated by the arrow reduces costs, but remains far above the (negative) cost of energy efficiency initiatives.

Cost of abatement

Energy efficiency   Community solar PV   Household solar PV

Private Investment Motives

In the private sector there are many reasons *that have nothing to do with emissions reduction* for the materialization of climate friendly investments. These could be:

- Rising fossil fuel prices
  - Rising fossil fuel prices will promote energy efficiency investments
- Security of supply
  - The supply of pipeline gas, for example, could be uncertain and be replaced by alternative captive energy sources
- Corporate Social Responsibility (CSR)
  - A climate friendly investment will respond to CSR goals and provide a positive image
- Energy access
  - Remote production bases could choose standalone alternative energy
- 'Real' environment
  - Cleaning up waste streams from the production might have positive spill-over effects on emissions
- Industrial policy
  - A national industrial policy promotes the development and deployment of a certain technology, e.g., wind energy
- Technology development
  - Due to positive market expectations manufacturers invest in improving or deploying cutting edge climate friendly technology
- Regulation
  - A simple response to regulation like energy efficiency standards
- *So ein Ding müssen wir auch haben ...*[4]
  - The neighbouring factory's installation of a large solar PV system might be a driver of investment

The private sector has always regarded emissions as an externality to production. The environment is free until a regulator puts a price on it and enforces his regulation. These days, corporations realize that there are limits beyond regulation that are set by civil society, which are responded to through corporate social responsibility (CSR) strategies. This created the voluntary carbon market, which did not experience the same free fall as the compliance market in 2012, mainly because it did not sell the emissions reduction, per se, but rather the context in which the emissions reduction materializes – i.e., the 'story'.

Apart from this there is no reason for the private sector to invest in emissions reduction, while there are many reasons to invest in things that have emissions reduction co-benefits – as long as they align with core business. Most of the motives listed above are driven by considerations for the core production, with a few exceptions: regulation, CSR, and energy efficiency. But regulation is circumvented or 'rent-seeked' against, CSR is ultimately promotion of sales, and energy efficiency investments rarely happen. Energy efficiency investments represent by far the cheapest emissions reduction options. However, despite their obvious profitability corporations generally devote their investment capital to securing their market position rather than reducing the cost of energy, unless it becomes crucial for competitiveness.

Bringing the private sector on board is about aligning initiatives with their core business.[5] Generic alignment with general industrial interests might be challenging, but sector specific initiatives are feasible. Such initiatives could be targeted reductions of import duty for certain types of energy efficient equipment, e.g., energy efficient furnaces. It quickly becomes clear, however, that the private sector reacts to not much other than public sector regulations – whether incentives, disincentives or hard regulations. Otherwise, the driver is the market and the corporate strategic response.

There seems to be a hope among some observers and organizations that the private sector's investment strategies, decisions and motivations could, and should, somehow be altered towards a sustainable development agenda – the CSR agendas seemingly not sufficiently anchored in the business community, as a whole. The UNEP Finance Initiative cites KPMG International's Corporate Sustainability progress report from 2011 (UNEP FI, 2012): 'Despite all the progress that has been made, more than a third of businesses still do not have a sustainability strategy in place. Of those that do, only one in three is reporting publicly on their progress.' This translates into about 10 per cent of businesses that report on sustainability indicators. UNEP FI believes that 'finance sector practitioners, professionals and other key decision makers such as pension fund trustee boards do not always have an understanding of sustainability issues', implying that once they do, investment decisions will change. They will not, however, unless it reflects on shareholders' value generation. This does not mean that businesses do not understand sustainability, but that the markets and their investors do not adequately value sustainability, including climate change, to bring about the kind of investments that are needed to meet the objectives of emissions reduction. The markets have not even come to grips with the true (negative) value of 'unburnable carbon'.[6]

The answer to the climate challenge lies in the interaction between the public and private sectors. If the market does not put an adequate value on sustainability, violating sustainability criteria remains an externality, or a 'market failure', and the corrective action then becomes the responsibility of the regulator. Hoping that the private sector will eventually 'understand sustainability' is not the answer, at least not in the short term.

Based on the above, it is clear that NAMAs are not necessarily funded as 'NAMAs', but as the substance of the initiative – a waste collection and disposal system; an efficient lighting programme; a CSR strategy or security of energy supply. It is, therefore, acceptable to fit existing policies or projects in under the NAMA label, highlighting the mitigation qualities of the initiative, but, for financing purposes, remaining conscious about fundamental financing requirements. Hence, NAMAs do not fall in a category that defies fundamental investment criteria.

The idealized linkage between different levels of policymaking in NAMA host countries, as illustrated in Figure 1, may eventually evolve. If so, these will be helpful in bringing about NAMAs that are founded on long-term priorities, represent coherent policies, and ultimately underpin the longer investment horizons that are particularly necessary for many capital-intensive low carbon technologies. The NAMA, by nature, can be a return to healthy basics in financing of emissions reduction actions with an active participation, including financial participation, of the private sector.

Summing Up

NAMA finance does not have an official definition, but agreeing on one would be useful. Without it not only will there be confusion about the numbers; there will also be confusion about its deployment. The 100 billion dollar mark is rather arbitrary and could be anything between very insufficient and quite adequate depending on what is meant, what is counted, and how it is used. If as here defining it as – the financing that must be engineered in order to allow the private sector *and* its banking partners to do their business as usual – it could well be sufficient. The NAMA finance is the leverag*ing* finance, in whichever form it is injected, and *not* the leverag*ed* finance. For all intents and purposes this leveraging finance is public.

It has also been argued that investment motivations for NAMAs have changed as compared to the CDM. While the CDM unsuccessfully advocated making the emissions reduction externality an investment driver the NAMA balances the true benefits of an investment with its emissions reduction benefit – the latter being a co-benefit. For the NAMA financier, who may still be driven by the emissions reduction perspective, the true benefit is a much healthier motivation on the part of the NAMA host, as the NAMA is fundamentally addressing not an externality, but a core development preference.

Chapter 5

THE FINANCING TOOLS . . .

In the previous chapter it was established that NAMA financing is a *public sector activity*. This may be at odds with the general understanding, but it is helpful in clarifying which financing is being referred to, and helps in shaping the financing landscape for NAMAs. Notably, it also clarifies which financing is *not* being referred to – for instance, not the billions of renminbi that are being invested in Chinese wind power, nor the billions that are being channelled through to African hydropower. It is not the energy efficiency investments in the cement industry, or any other profitable efficiency investments in other industries, either. Instead, NAMA financing is the public sector 'contribution' that ensures these investments take place, and that they do so on the basis of otherwise normal profitability considerations.

It is how public sector financing is injected into the system that constitutes the financial engineering of NAMAs. There are many instruments available to the public sector, and they are quite traditional. It is not so much about inventing new instruments, as it is about using the existing ones in new and possibly unexplored ways. Sometimes it is about challenging the mandates given to public sector financing institutions (see Chapter 8).

As indicated in Table 1 (Chapter 2), some of the instruments need not be financial – which could challenge the above definition. 'Hard' regulation, e.g., imposing efficiency investments in industry, has no financing implications for the regulator, if the entire investment is imposed on the private sector, and no grants, financing model or instrument is offered. In the case of energy efficiency, most of such investments would be profitable, when seen in isolation. From an incremental cost consideration based on calculations of the net present value, the incremental cost is negative and, thus, no climate finance will have gone into it. That is a disturbing conclusion, particularly because these investments for the private sector will occupy financing capital that otherwise would have been prioritized for investment in core business – the prime reason for omitting profitable efficiency investments in the industry in the first place.

So, does the definition need to be altered? No. There is a tendency to label all investments, capital and financing, which may result in emissions reduction, as 'climate finance'. That inflates the term. The result will either be an exaggeration of the momentous task at hand, or it will be a claim that the 100 billion dollar mark has been reached by counting billions of dollars that have nothing to do with climate finance. If one were to count those efficiency investments that are imposed, how should one count, not to mention record, those that are not imposed, but happen regardless? The lesson learnt from the CDM is clearly to refrain from interpreting the motivations behind investments as a means to determine whether the investment is an emissions reduction one or not.

There may be cases, however, where an investment in the private sector, imposed through hard regulation by the public regulator, is *not* profitable and has an actual incremental cost – the net present value of the investment, negative. Does that require NAMA finance? Yes, it does. Such investments are traditionally imposed through the setting of standards. In housing, for instance, the trend is to raise efficiency standards. In the lower end of the spectrum, such standards impose profitable improvements of the building envelope. For instance, it is a good idea to introduce window glazing instead of wooden shutters in climates that require air conditioning. It would be profitable at almost any subsidized electricity price. At the other end of the spectrum, zero-energy housing would be profitable only at highly taxed energy prices. The increased cost of construction would require climate finance – either for the construction, or to pay the energy taxes. However, in countries where the latter is relevant, i.e., in the most developed economies, the additional cost of construction is not counted as climate investment – and neither are the energy taxes. It is a condition precedent.

The transition to such a situation, however, may require climate finance. The transformational change that is called for in NAMAs, aims exactly at accelerating the development in a sector towards a new, more efficient and more sustainable conduct. Imposing standards that go beyond profitability may require financing schemes supported by the government or by international financing institutions, in the form of NAMAs. That is where the NAMA finance materializes.

This could be regarded as a conservative approach to defining NAMA finance, but it is practical, and avoids battles over which part of the private sector's investments should be counted, and which should not. The private sector's investments, both national and international, have manifold motivations, as listed in the previous chapter, with almost all having a profit motive. The NAMA finance activating the private sector is meant to support such profit motives.

It is not at all certain, however, whether the activity in question for a NAMA involves the private sector. In the large majority of both developing and developed countries, the energy sector is publicly owned. Currently, development institutions are devoting 47 per cent of their climate-related financing to the energy sector. Another 34 per cent is going into transport, which is also a typical public sector activity.

Figure 7. Multilateral investment in mitigation and typical instruments employed

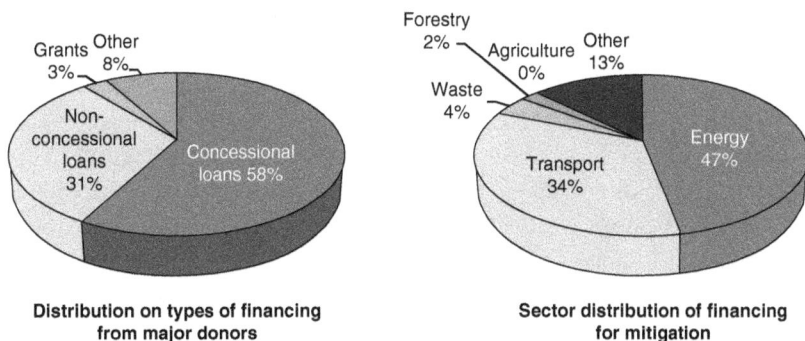

**Distribution on types of financing
from major donors**

**Sector distribution of financing
for mitigation**

Source: *Accessing International Financing for Climate Change Mitigation – A Guidebook for Developing Countries.* Left pie based on data from JICA, KfW, AfD and EIB (original source Stockholm Environment Institute, 2009).

NAMA finance does not require private sector involvement, per se. It can focus on public sector entities alone, in corporatized but still publicly owned structures. Such approaches are likely to be common in NAMAs due to the strategic characteristics, particularly of the energy sector, but it means that a significant financing capability in the private sector is not activated. Therefore, if the private sector is to play a role in raising investment capital for climate friendly investments, one of the first considerations when planning a NAMA must be to determine a possibly expanded role of the private sector.

The private involvement in infrastructure in the 1990s did not leave a uniformly positive track record, and the predominantly Asian financial crisis in 1998 returned the investment levels to their starting point of 10 years earlier. However, since then, significant developments in financing trends have produced a healthier environment for public–private collaborations on the financing of different types of infrastructure (Kingombe, 2011). The Overseas Development Institute (ODI) estimates that in 2009 the main hybrid Development Finance Institutions (publicly supported investors operating on private sector principles, see Chapter 7) invested approximately USD 33 billion in the private sector – in the form of loans, guarantees and equity positions – most of which went to infrastructure and the financial sector. The International Finance Corporation (IFC) under the World Bank and the European Bank for Reconstruction and Development (EBRD) were the largest investors.

When the public sector wants to promote such investment by the private sector it has a number of instruments at its disposal. Figure 8 (recapturing part of Table 1) is a quite exhaustive list of options, effectively constituting a preliminary typology for NAMAs (UNEP Risø, 2011). The listed instruments, here called *operational* instruments, may be orchestrated by a NAMA host; his ability to do so is ultimately decisive for the success of the NAMA. Leaving this to the NAMA hosts alone is risky, not because of the lack of will or interest, but because this may be a discipline that some NAMA developers in line ministries are either unfamiliar with or approach with a traditional donor–recipient mind-set. Aggregators that can help orchestrate the instruments, and the financiers behind them, are what is needed (see Chapters 8 and 9).

The operational instruments that the public sector has at its disposal can be categorized along three interlinked dimensions. The first fundamental differentiation is between investment and cash flow, or investment and operational budgets. Public investment budgets are typically financed through one-time appropriations on the national budget, possibly involving loan financing. It has the advantage over recurrent spending that it does not require a permanent budget commitment in following fiscal years, unless the investment requires an operational budget once completed. Such recurrent spending requires financing through recurrent income, typically taxes.

The second differentiation is between the instruments which have budgetary consequences for the regulator and instruments that do not. The latter is often sector specific regulation that puts the burden of finance on the sector itself (although part of the activities in the sector may be public). These are for instance building codes, energy efficiency standards and labelling requirements for low GHG products. They are not included in the table. The financing instruments are the delivery system for the part of the financial architecture that is controlled by the public sector, i.e. the NAMA finance, the purpose of which is to change incentives and disincentives towards a more sustainable conduct in a given sector.

The third dimension is the financing products and the sources of such financing (see following chapter) that the public sector can engage to finance these regulatory instruments. In Figure 8 these are called *sourcing* instruments. This financing can either be channelled through, or arranged by, the public sector for the benefit of the private sector, who's financing instruments, also listed in Figure 8, may be enhanced through public sector intervention. Figure 8 further relates the instruments to the definition of NAMA financing from Figure 5, illustrating which elements are generally inside the NAMA financing architecture and which ones are left to the private sector for its 'business-as-usual' financing approaches. The sourcing instruments listed in Figure 8 are described in the following.

Public Sector Sourcing Instruments

The sourcing instruments refer to the upstream financing efforts that are required for the initial establishment of a budgetary foundation for the

Figure 8. Sourcing instruments and operational instruments for NAMA financing

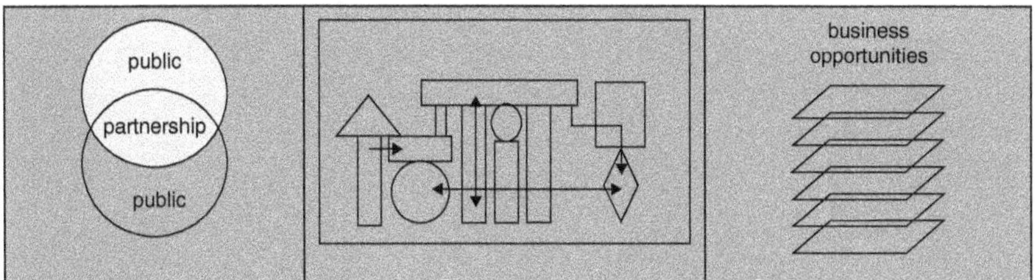

Public sector sourcing instruments	Public sector operational instruments	Private sector financing instruments
Environmental Fiscal Reform	Grants	Equity
Loans	Purchase contracts for goods	First-loss (mezzanine, junior debt)
Soft loans	Purchase contracts for services	
Bonds	Additional payments (e.g. feed-in tariffs)	Loans
Dedicated credit lines	Public procurement guidelines	Bonds
Risk cover, guarantees	Tax credits, reductions/exemptions	Risk cover, guarantees
Grants	Variable or accelerated depreciations	Project finance
	Removing subsidies	Grants
	Loan schemes	
	Guarantee schemes	

development of a NAMA. Their basis is either domestic public or international public, although in some instances loan models may also be developed together with the private banking sector, be it domestic in the NAMA host country or internationally.

Environmental Fiscal Reform

It has been established, also by the 'official' guidance on NAMA development, that the starting point for raising financing for NAMAs is the national budget. In that regard NAMA host countries may seek inspiration in 'Environmental Fiscal Reform' (EFR), its relevance growing from M3 to M1 countries following the curve in Figure 2. EFR is a tax reform aiming at 'getting prices right' through the levying of taxes in order to 'internalize externalities'. As the ultimate responsibility for designing regulative compliance structures rests with national governments, the choices they make – through their prerogative to draft national (tax) policies – have direct and indirect consequences for the preferences in a given sector in terms of investment in and operation of equipment with varying emission profiles.[1]

'Getting prices right' implies that the true cost of production is not reflected in current prices (however theoretical that calculation would have to be). Externalities are normally only regulated against once they become unacceptable by the public. In most situations the inability of prices to pay the true environmental costs means that other sources of finance are employed by default. There are three identifiable sources discussed in the following:

1) Prices on products and services
2) Taxes paid by present tax-payers
3) Taxes paid by future tax-payers

Any undistributed cost continues to be carried by the free and available environment.

Prices on products and services

Distinguishing between prices and present tax-payers as sources of finance is somewhat superficial, as both avenues of revenue generation reflect taxes, but they do not have equal behavioural effects. Pricing environmental damage may be done directly or indirectly, either reflected through charging environmental taxes on (retail) products, ensuring that the consumer pays, or through taxing production – which sooner or later ends up as a price to be paid by the consumer as illustrated in Figure 9. The benefit of this is that the consumer can relate to the price paid for consumption of the environment (depending on the successful demonstration of the relation).

In practice there are several aspects that the NAMA host must consider before deciding on a tax structure:

1) Current taxation of the item
Environmental taxes are already employed as fiscal instruments – in some NAMA host countries more than others. This commonness may ensure acceptability of the instrument by the regulated, but he may also feel that he is already paying for 'environment consumption'. In some, although mainly developed countries the environmental taxes have already been used far beyond the environmental cost – but nothing prevents the regulator from moving beyond the 'pigouvian' level and tax above the environmental cost.

2) Indifference
If the intention behind the tax is emissions reduction, taxation must alter the consumer's behaviour. If it does not, i.e., if the consumer is indifferent to (increased) taxes (e.g., increased petrol prices that does not immediately change the need for transportation), only the revenue increases. Emissions are unchanged. Hence, from the regulators point of view, 'getting the prices right' in the meaning that prices reflect the true environmental cost of production, does not necessarily bring about the behavioural changes needed to achieve

Figure 9. Direct and indirect taxation

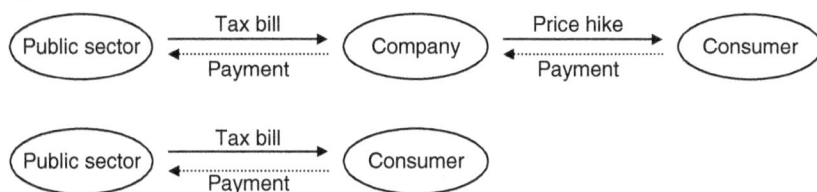

emissions reduction. For instance, only an average of 2 to 3 per cent of the retail value of products in general stem from energy costs. Growing energy prices therefore only affect general prices insignificantly and increasing carbon taxes even less so.

3) Revenue preservation
Indifference, of course, is good for revenue preservation. Nevertheless, the revenue already generated by taxing the item must follow an accumulation curve that eventually peaks, i.e., that the reduced total consumption brings in less tax than a higher consumption with a lower tax. The optimum taxation level is fully detached from the actual environmental cost and depends only on the consumed items' indispensability, i.e., if it lacks substitutes.

The overall challenge to EFR is that it depends on continued consumption of the taxed good. If a country, e.g., depends on revenues from energy taxes and exempts renewable energy from tax to promote the phasing out of fossil fuels, the tax bureau will eventually need to tax the desired renewable alternative as net energy tax revenues starts declining.

4) Recycling
If a sector, like the energy sector, produces an indispensable good, taxing the production according to true environmental cost may be softened by recycling part of the revenue back into the sector to remedy part of the loss of competitiveness. This is in essence the purpose of the EFR – to generate revenues that can be deployed in a manner that changes behaviour. But if recycled revenues reward the efficient performers, the recycling of revenues back into the taxed sector might just add insult to injury for those inefficient producers who may exist in remote areas where, e.g., local employment considerations could weigh more heavily than reducing emissions. In such cases cross-subsidization may be a more attractive option.

5) Competition
The regulator is not free to choose his package of instruments. He may have domestic competition interests in mind, not altering the balance

of competition too significantly, but more importantly he probably faces international competition which limits the level to which he can raise domestic environmental taxes.

The relations between these issues are not straightforward, and it is never as black and white. The fine tuning of the regulatory system should aim at balancing the positive and negative forces to achieve as much environmental improvement as possible within the 'pain tolerances' of the regulated.

Present tax-payers

The alternative to impose direct taxes on 'use of the environment' is to impose a generic tax, i.e., paying the environmental costs through the state budget and financing it through general tax revenues. For regulators (governments), this is one way out of the problem of taxing corporate entities out of the country. The down-side of this approach is its lack of behavioural effects as consumers and corporations are not faced with any cost specifically related to their 'use of the environment'. It is the flipside of the notion that the private sector will have to contribute to the financing of emissions reduction without being taxed to do so.

General taxes effectively distribute the cost of emissions reduction on all economic sectors. In cap-and-trade systems for the industry the government could tender tight quotas and recycle the revenues back into the emitting industries by rolling back other taxes as compensation. In that manner, the corporations will ensure the emissions reduction, while other tax-payers, through generic taxes, could secure the financing. If the corporations are not compensated by rolling back other taxes, putting restrictive quotas corresponds to letting the prices carry the cost as described above. Having to increase prices is the overall concern of any potentially emission capped entity; the more so in sectors with global competition in linked markets. Separate markets on the other hand may succeed in sustaining price differences.

Future tax-payers

Naturally, any present action could be left for future generations to pay for, simply by abstaining from raising taxes, but this is not what is meant by 'future tax-payers'. By 'future tax-payers' is meant 'future action'. It implies a budget approach and an undetermined bill for future tax-payers. Its attractiveness is based on the assumption that technology will improve and help carry the emissions reduction burden, despite the burden having grown in the meantime. It has current tax-payers off the hook. Upholding uncertainty as to how or by whom or to what extent the burden is to be carried in the future only influences current behaviour if the threat is perceived real and quantifiable.

Non-domestic sources

EFR fundamentally concerns an activation of national financing capabilities for the establishment of a full or partial economic foundation for a NAMA. The remaining sourcing instruments listed in Figure 8 originate from external sources, either national or international. All, with the exception of grants, are loan models with more or less favourable repayment terms. They will be addressed in the following chapters linked to the institutions that provide them or to the financial engineering principles that underpin the NAMA.

Public Sector Operational Instruments

Many instruments that are relevant sourcing instruments are equally relevant as operational instruments. Particularly those that relate to EFR, which concern both the inward revenues from taxation as well as the possibility for outward subsidies in support of preferred behaviour in the market.

Grants

In the rearranging of the public budget in an environmental fiscal reform there is a natural overlap between the instruments available for financing the public sector intervention and the instruments available for the public sector to inspire the transformational changes that the NAMA is to deliver. Many of them represent public sector support for certain preferred actions and as such, therefore may be regarded as grants offered by the NAMA host country's regulatory authorities. Grants take different forms. They can be linked to the purchase of equipment, e.g., a grant offered for the purchase of more energy efficient air conditioner or, as, e.g., the Mauritian government has practiced, grants for the purchase of solar water heating units. It is less common to think of feed-in tariffs as grants, although in practice they correspond to paying an additional fee for a desired service. Fossil fuel subsidies are in effect also grants, although more for desired services (transportation and energy supply) with *un*desired side effects (greenhouse gas emissions). The feed-in tariff is the most common example, where an existing tariff is topped-up with an additional payment for a low emission energy supply from e.g. wind turbines, solar PV, hydropower or biomass. In Figure 8 the feed-in tariff is called 'additional payments'. They are in fact akin to GEFs incremental costs approach, but directed towards operating costs as opposed to capital costs.

Grants in one form or another are offered by the public sector to incentivise private sector investment. Such investments may be desirable from different perspectives. In the Mauritian case one of the purposes was to reduce the demand for additional central power generation capacity. The feed-in tariff, typically offered to independent power producers, may be motivated by security of supply through the diversification of the energy base; by a desire to support a national equipment supplies industry, or by an objective to convert a public investment burden into a private service supply and thus (additional) public recurrent spending for, e.g., continuous service that does not require any grants, e.g., the supply of electricity or water on market terms or the operation of a waste collection system. Contracts may also be for the purchase of a one-time service, e.g., the cleaning up of a landfill, a coal mine or other large installations, where emissions can be controlled. Such contracts may also be based on a one-time grant.

Taxes

The above pertains to the outflow of cash, as opposed to investment capital. The inflow of cash also represents options for incentivising desirable actions in the private sector. A tax credit, for instance, can take many forms, but generally refers to tax holidays, e.g. a five-year tax holiday for power generation investments, as was adopted in India, together with other tax-based promotions, like accelerated depreciation.[2] Combined, such instruments may, in practice, render desired installations tax free in the initial years of operation, where the risks are perceived as high among investors. Clearly, tax revenues are lost and may need to be recovered.

Removal of subsidies is particularly relevant in relation to fossil fuel. It is one of the most obvious sources of finance for other climate friendly investments, but it has shown remarkable resilience in the face of growing pressure for emissions reduction. In September 2009, the leaders of the Group of Twenty (G-20) countries agreed to phase out inefficient fossil fuel subsidies over the medium term. This amounts to USD 312 billion worldwide. Moreover, 95 per cent of the current growth in oil demand comes from countries where the oil price is subject to subsidies (IEA World Energy Outlook, 2010). The IEA estimates that removing fossil fuel consumption subsidies would reduce global carbon dioxide emissions by 1.5 to 2 billion tonnes, by 2020. Removal, or rather an initial restructuring, of such subsidies could (and probably should) be one of the important sources of national co-financing when international finance is sought. Their continuation would be one of the most obvious obstacles to the desired investments in emission free alternatives. While the private sector is indifferent to these subsidies, if their NAMA promoted emission free investment can be hedged against them, the donor financiers may see it as a thorn in the side to commit (scarce) climate finance for competing with subsidy schemes that predominantly benefit the wealthier parts of the NAMA host country. Nevertheless, the fossil fuel subsidies are likely to remain a sore spot for a little while longer.

Loans and guarantees

Loan schemes are the provision of loans, possibly on concessional terms, i.e., below market rates, for projects with emissions reduction qualities. However, it may also be the making available of loan funding on alternative platforms like government backed green bonds issuance. Loan schemes may also include programmes for subordinated, 'first-loss' loans in different loan structures (like PEBBLE structures introduced in Chapter 9). Loan structures will remain the largest part of the financial engineering of NAMAs. More importantly, however, while the loan is used for the financing of capital goods, it is the debt service that is essential in the financial engineering of the NAMA – the asset's ability to return the financing.

The most common reason for project financing to not come together is that the risk/return ratio is not attractive. In January 2013, the Climate Policy Initiative (CPI) launched a series of risk gap analyses stating that 'currently, gaps in risk coverage hinder renewable energy investments. Risk — whether real or perceived — is in fact the single most important factor preventing renewable energy projects from finding financial investors, or raising the returns that these investors demand. It is also one thing that policymakers can cause, control, alleviate, or help mitigate.'[3]

Guarantees are playing central roles at all levels, with guarantee models designed to provide the necessary confidence among those financiers that balance the price of their money against the risk of losing it. Even financiers that have lost the capital up front, by providing a grant, are considering the risk of not getting value for money. That, of course, requires an operational asset. Guarantees help, not only in bringing together the capital in the first place, but also in reducing the price of it, extending the patience of it, and increasing the reach of it. This applies to loans, in some cases subordinated loans, to equity and cash flows. The employment of a guarantee is most often used for the enhancement of a cash flow, with the exception of an investment guarantee – although even the investment guarantee is to ensure the investor's payback through continuous returns on the investment.

The challenge for financing in many NAMA host countries becomes evident when studying Figure 10 – which illustrates the cost of additional risk cover in developing countries compared to the same cost in a developed country. The difference is striking – real and perceived risks almost tripling the financing costs. If risks triple the cost of capital, project activities in NAMA host countries will require a corresponding additional income. The reality is that, more often than not, there is additional competition from fossil fuel subsidies. Concessional elements in the financing structure are obviously needed, but reducing the risk or eliminating risk elements should be the immediate and first response – and, therefore, also the prime instrument in NAMA financing structures – if they involve private sector financing. This ultimately means that NAMA financing consists of the cost of providing the finance at conditions that are not commensurate with the real and perceived risks in the particular NAMA host country, i.e., typical concessional financing.

Most often, if the NAMA host engages in any of these instruments, it will not host the instrument itself – with the exception of tax holidays or other tax incentives that must be managed by the tax authorities. Loans with or without concessional elements will typically be extended to private sector entities through a national development bank (for example, the Mauritian government loans to households' purchase of solar water heaters through the Mauritian Development Bank during the 2000s).

What happened to the carbon credit?

There are niches where the international carbon credit may survive, like in Japan's Bilateral Offset Crediting Mechanism which deploys Japanese low-carbon technology and products in partner countries in order to calculate, evaluate and bring home credits contributing to meeting Japan's self-imposed reduction target. It does so, however, as a distinct alternative to the international carbon market – not as a contribution to it. But under the Partnership for Market Readiness (PMR)[4] the World Bank is 'shaping the next generation of carbon markets…' In the beginning of 2013, 16 countries representing close to 40 per cent of global emissions were set on a path to develop their market readiness plans, of which Chile, China, Costa Rica and Mexico were already moving ahead with implementation.

Those that still dream of an international carbon market regard this development as a fragmentation of the market. It happens, however, against a backdrop of a possible overhang of 1.3 billion CERs from the CDM during the period 2013–15 and another 2.1 billion during 2016–20 (Michaelowa, 2012). To absorb the overhang large scale programmes of voluntary retirement of

Figure 10. Cost of types of risk

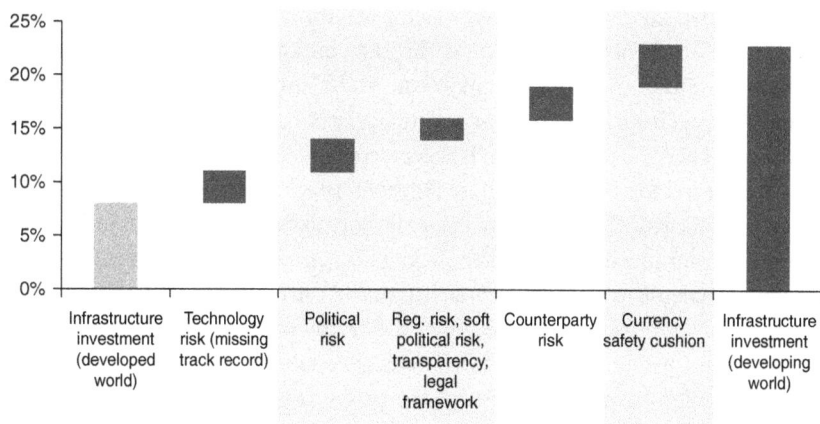

Source: DB Climate Change Advisors.

CERs are required in response either to the UNFCCC Secretariats invitation to submit CERs for voluntary cancellation (576,000 CERs by the end of 2013) or through CER sales to some national CER purchase programmes (e.g., Norway in 2013, Sweden in 2014 and NEFCO in 2013).

The voluntary carbon credit has shown much more resilience to the financial crisis than the compliance credit. Used carefully, it could become a platform for rewarding NAMAs on a credit and, thus, cash flow basis without introducing a formalized off-setting mechanism for developed country commitments. It could also become a source of domestic cash flow. As the reverse engineering of the CDM in Chapter 2 suggests finance can be engineered around such cash flows if they are sufficiently secure and the carbon 'cap-and-trade' scheme under which it might exist has sufficient safeguards to protect it against market and price collapse.

The certainty and durability of the cap needs to be trusted by the actors in the system. An enforcement system sufficiently strong to ensure compliance must accompany the scheme.[5] The system should be guarded from inclusion of default offsets from activities that are not driven by emissions reduction motives. The European Emission Trading System (EU ETS) has failed here, although it mostly (but not entirely) emulated the UNFCCC eligibility criteria for CDM activities. It should also have built-in control mechanisms to keep a reasonable supply/demand balance within a pre-defined band to avoid stop-go decision drivers for long-term investments like energy infrastructure. The EU ETS has failed here as well. And finally it should be based on long-term commitments, even long-term contracts between emitter and regulator, for the off-sets or reductions to be delivered – agreements that are comparable to investment horizons within a given sector. Once again, the EU ETS has failed, auctioning allowances for the short to medium term only.

If such ills cannot be prevented through national regulation it is a valid question whether they can be guaranteed by anyone in the market. It is imaginable that insurances against non-delivery of carbon credits can be aligned with general performance bonds. It is even conceivable that guarantees, parallel to those offered for Power Purchase Agreements (PPAs) between independent power producers and government owned transmission companies, could secure long-term contracts based on off-set/reduction agreements between an emitter and a national government. It is not straightforward, however, to guarantee the durability of an off-set regime per se and thus the continuation of the demand for the emissions reduction. These considerations primarily pertain to the potential foreign investor, who is not the prime target of a national emissions trading scheme. National carbon markets are for national emitters and foreign investors will regard them as a framework condition along with other parameters in their investment decisions. It is therefore likely that the concerns raised will be dismissed by the local emission constrained industry, which is accustomed to working in the national context, and is in a better position to evaluate the political context.

The national cap-and-trade regimes are by far less complicated than the international ones, as the regulatory regime will be under (relative) control, and enforcement structures can be established. The underlying cap may be efficient in achieving emissions reduction, but this is not guaranteed. Opening the gates for imports (from zero-cost, default credit production regimes) is tempting when regulated emitters start complaining, which remains a latent risk in any such regime, potentially reducing its emissions reduction effect. Until that happens, however, it may be an efficient way to raise local capital from the emitting industry.

A 'hijacking' of the NAMA could also be the voluntary credit's way into formalization in a new climate regime. A NAMA-based on the implementation of a system that, either project or sector wise, calculates and issues carbon credits on the basis of performance – employing for instance CDM methodologies – would be in conformity with the World Bank's PMR strategy. Moreover, it would produce a credit that can either be applied in a national cap and trade system, or it could exploit, or be exploited by, the current voluntary credit standards like the Gold Standard and the Voluntary Carbon Standard (VCS), which are, in fact, much better suited to the NAMA due to their independence of international agreements. They can exploit corporate interests in certain types of carbon credits, mainly driven by CSR considerations, or they could make a pitch towards the C40 Cities Climate Leadership group, that could in turn establish their own internal demand models for certain types of voluntary credits. Vietnam, for instance, is already considering post-2020 strategies to build emission reduction projects for the voluntary carbon market.

Summing Up

The tools available to leverage the financing of NAMAs are first and foremost public sector regulation. The regulation has two functions. On one side it is to raise the financing upon which the NAMA is to rest. Environmental fiscal reform may help bringing about such financing. On the other side the regulation is about establishing such regulatory incentives that make investments happen. One of the tools not utilized to its full potential is risk cover. The other important instrument is cash flow, preferably the predictable kind that can support private sector investment. So far, the carbon credits that have experienced a crashing market are the only source of climate change related cash flows that have been seen in prospective NAMA host countries, but the numerous other cash flows controlled by the public sector through taxes, including carbon taxes, or payments for services are equally relevant and useful. A number of other instruments will each play their role in the financing landscape. They are not sources of NAMA financing themselves, but may be vehicles through which the NAMA financing can be injected. Equity and mezzanine financing, for instance, are private sector instruments that may be enhanced through, e.g., favourable tax rules offered by the NAMA host. However, while the tools are known, the sources of their possible funding, if not purely from the NAMA host country's national budget, are diverse. The following chapter is devoted to the financiers.

Chapter 6

. . . AND THE FINANCIERS

To engineer the financing of a NAMA it is necessary to know which financing tools and which financiers are already in the market. Various institutions offer different sets of tools – although some new NAMA institutions claim that they provide any tool as required. When drafting ideas for NAMAs it is tempting to assume that this new concept, which is not an instrument, will also come with a new source of funding – preferably grant funding flowing from the deep pockets of a prospective Green Climate Fund. However, the large majority of the funding for the investments promoted by NAMAs will come from other, well-known sources and will be employing well-known principles that are *not* grants. That does not mean that all the tools are at hand to financially engineer all promising and visionary NAMA options.

Financing and financing institutions have been central to the UNFCCC since its inception. The UNFCCC was originally brought about with a financial mechanism – the Global Environment Facility (GEF) – which has been providing financing for a multitude of projects over the years. Established in 1991, it has the longest track record of all institutions financing climate change mitigation and adaptation programmes and projects. GEF enjoys a partnership with 10 agencies, including the major international development banks as well as FAO, IFAD, UNEP, UNIDO and UNDP – supporting not only climate change, but also a range of other environmental agendas. GEF provides grants for projects on the basis of the documentation of incremental costs affiliated with a low emissions alternative, compared to a business as usual choice. About 33 per cent (or USD 1.14 billion) of GEF's Fifth Replenishment, from 2010–2014, was dedicated to climate change, aiming to reduce 500 million tonnes of CO_2e. By 1 July 2012, GEF had invested in 569 climate change mitigation projects, since 1991, contributing USD 3.6 billion as co-financing to total investments of USD 27.3 billion. Thus, GEF's average financial involvement in the climate change mitigation projects was about 13 per cent – signalling a relatively small incremental cost in most projects.

While GEF's track record is impressive, it is a far cry from the USD 100 billion target for developed countries' annual contribution to climate change actions in developing countries. To raise and channel this amount to climate-related investments, the Conference of the Parties in Cancun, in 2010, decided to establish the Green Climate Fund (GCF). Making the fund operational, however – and capitalizing the fund – is a slow process; unfortunately so slow that some bilateral donor agencies have initiated their own financing structures. The GCF negotiations have been delayed due to fundamental differences in perspective, mainly concerning the expectations for the composition of the funding and the modalities for its deployment. Although it is a grey scale, the main divide is between developing countries that see the USD 100 billion figure enshrined in Cancun as a target for annual developed country public sector budget allocations transferred to the GCF, and handed out as grants for climate-change-related projects, and most developed countries that emphasize that the figure is a target for the entire mobilization of funds from developed countries, be it public or private sector, grants or re-payable loans, or other financing instruments that accumulate into the USD 100 billion figure. The latter is clearly in conflict with the definition of NAMA finance adopted in this book (but then again the GCF is not targeted specifically at NAMAs).

The GCF has been headquartered in Seoul, South Korea. Its 24 member Board govern the GCF on the basis of a business model adopted in August 2012,[1] stating that 'The Fund will promote the paradigm shift towards low-emission and climate-resilient development pathways by providing support to developing countries, striving to maximize the impact of its funding for adaptation and mitigation, and seeking a balance between the two. Its operations will be country-driven and it will promote and strengthen engagement at the country level through effective involvement of relevant institutions and stakeholders. ... The ambition of the Fund is to become the main global fund for climate change finance and to catalyse additional public and private finance at the international and national levels. The GCF modalities and procedures are still being discussed.'[2]

The catalysing of financing from different sources is a central objective. Catalysing, or leveraging, funds from other sources is what the financial engineering of NAMAs is about, and the following chapter is dedicated to this exercise. But who, or what, is leveraging what? In the above formulation, it is indicated that the GCF will take it upon itself to leverage funding from other sources, both public and private. This seems not to be adopted in a similar fashion by those bilateral 'NAMA financing institutions' that have emerged.

The most important of these is the NAMA Facility, which was launched at COP18 in Doha in 2012 and made operational in 2013, jointly by the German Federal Ministry for the Environment, Nature Conservation and

Nuclear Safety, and the United Kingdom Department of Energy and Climate Change. According to the programme website, it 'is designed to support developing countries that show leadership on tackling climate change and want to implement transformational country-led NAMAs'. It is capitalized with an initial EUR 70 million (EUR 40 million from Germany's Special Energy and Climate Fund, and GBP 25 million from the UK Government's funding of the International Climate Fund) that may be applied in the form of grants, concessional loans and guarantees. Proponents must document full endorsement by the relevant national line ministry or agency for the implementation of the activity covered by the NAMA proposal. In the first round of applications, five projects were selected for in-depth appraisal[3] to determine the activities that the NAMA Facility will ultimately invest in through its main delivery channels: the KfW Development Bank and Deutsche Gesellschaft für Internationale Zusammenarbeit GmbH (GIZ).

The UNFCCC NAMA Registry (see Chapter 2) also contains a register for NAMA financiers who may announce their interest in providing finance for NAMAs. At the end of 2013, the register contained seven institutions, of which the NAMA Facility was one, and the GEF was another. The remaining five were:

Latin American Investment Facility
Neighbourhood Investment Facility
EU-Africa Infrastructure Trust Fund
Climate-related ODA funding
International Climate Initiative (IKI)

Of these, the last two are different arms of Germany's bilateral assistance programmes that redirect some of their activities towards NAMAs. The remaining three are EU-based. The EU-Africa Infrastructure Trust Fund (ITF) was established as a result of the Partnership on Infrastructure, launched in October 2007 by the African Union Commission (AUC) and the European Commission. Generally, it promotes investment in regional infrastructure in Africa, but 'in order for the EU to meet its commitments in terms of climate finance, specific Climate Change Windows (CCWs) have been created in EU regional blending mechanisms such as the ITF' (according to the NAMA Registry). Similar wording is used for the Latin American Investment Facility (LAIF) and the Neighbourhood Investment Facility (NIF), both of which are EU-based financing instruments that collaborate with other, primarily European, hybrid investment funds.

To some observers, this may bolster suspicion of non-additional funding being redirected towards NAMAs. Nevertheless, the implementation model for these EU-based instruments is noteworthy. 'The grant resources [of the Facilities] are blended with long-term loan financing from selected development finance institutions, helping to mobilize additional project finance and foster sustainable economic growth.' While co-financing is not uncommon – it is the rule rather than the exception – it indicates an active role of the LAIF, the NIF and the ITF in putting together the financing plan – a role that should be assumed by such aggregators for NAMA financing (see Chapters 8 and 9).

The above may indicate that specific NAMA financing institutions could be few and far between, but that does not need to be a negative thing. In fact, it is a good thing if it indicates that the existing financing instruments and institutions are becoming aware of the NAMA as an investment platform. These will ultimately be the ones from which the NAMA will leverage the bulk of the financing for climate-change-related projects.

In line with the addition of NAMAs to the EU funds' list of investment motivations, there are a multitude of additional funding structures and institutions that are relevant to the financial engineering of NAMAs, depending on scope and geography. These could include: the Least Developed Country Fund (LDCF) and the Special Climate Change Fund (SCCF) under the UNFCCC – which, combined, made up about 7.5 per cent of GEF's budget in the 4th financing cycle – or the two substantial Climate Investment Funds (CIF), the Clean Technology Fund (CTF) and the Strategic Climate Fund (SCF)[4], to which 14 countries have pledged over USD 6.5 billion – disbursed as grants, highly concessional loans, and/or risk mitigation instruments.

The following is neither a total account, nor a full description of all NAMA-relevant finance institutions. Such overviews have already been excellently produced by the ODI and Heinrich Böll Foundation (Caravani et al., 2012), and GEF and UNEP Risø (GEF/UNEP Risø, 2012). Rather, the following is an overview of the financing modalities that they represent, and their relevance to NAMA financing – although they do not explicitly finance NAMAs, per se, and maybe never will. The overview will help in establishing the gaps and identifying the tools that are either missing in the toolbox or seem misplaced, or else would be best moved or duplicated for other contexts.

The Institutional Investor

Many NAMAs relate to infrastructure in a broader sense: energy, transport, waste, water supply and waste water treatment. It is a common perception that infrastructure development and institutional investors, mainly pension funds, are a perfect match. Infrastructure requires long-term financing, while institutional investors are looking for long-term investments. Most of the climate finance is likely to go into larger scale infrastructure investments, which would also be valid for the NAMA. There may in addition be a multitude of smaller scale NAMAs that focus on smaller interventions that are not infrastructure related and will not attract large amounts of funds. These are not relevant investment objects for the institutional investor.

Institutional investors are portfolio investors with risk spreading strategies requiring both low risk and higher risk investments. Long-term finance for higher risk assets is, of course, a smaller proportion of the portfolio, but as climate-related investments are considered 'higher risk' and not 'too high risk' there is a place typically for renewable energy investments in these portfolios. Most of the motivation for this is the concern of corporate social responsibility (CSR), as these investors ultimately manage citizens' private savings – whether the funds administrators are government custodians or manage privately held pensions. Therefore, they are vulnerable to public discontent, resulting from the investment decisions – even though most prospective pensioners are likely more concerned with the size of their future pension than with the environment. The institutional investor, however, is rarely in possession of extensive resources for investment due diligence. Their risk assessments may, therefore, be relatively 'crude' – missing the niches of good quality investment options in less familiar investment climates. Thus, the NAMAs will rarely show on their radars.

There are ways to bridge the gap. The institutional investor may act as refinancier of existing or recently built assets. The refinancing approach avoids the significant initial risks in project development, construction and initial operation, while reducing the burden of due diligence to 'a check of the books', as the asset will have a performance record, and the institutional framework will have stood a first test. This strategy, of course, requires other better-suited development financiers to finance the initial investment, but it frees up these investors' capital for revolving project development.

There is still some way to go for the institutional investor, before he becomes the substantial contributor to bringing the NAMA financing together. The institutional investor would often engage a range of intermediary funds managers. In 2011, the Institutional Investors' Group on Climate Change, consisting of 80+ institutional investors representing approximately EUR 7.5 trillion of capital, analysed the importance of climate change among institutional investors and found that 78 per cent of asset owners now consider climate change integration when selecting funds managers, while 53 per cent monitor existing managers on climate issues.[5] However, to institutional investors, climate change is still mainly regarded as a risk, and the approaches to risk assessment 'vary between the asset classes in which investment is made.

Assessing climate risk for fixed assets such as real estate and infrastructure is generally focused on the potential physical impacts of climate change and/ or carbon emissions as an indicator of the energy efficiency of specific assets. For listed equities, carbon emissions are used to assess potential liabilities under carbon pricing or taxation schemes which will read through into (lower) company earnings and profits.' With this point of departure, getting the institutional investors and their Group on Climate Change from seeing climate change as a growing risk to their investment portfolio, to regarding it as an investment opportunity that even contributes (albeit, marginally) to reducing the climate risk to the traditional investment portfolio seems an outlandish, yet necessary step.

The Insurance Companies

If the world's most important investor community still regards climate change as mostly a risk, then risk insurance would be a natural place to look for another capital reserve to potentially activate in the financial engineering of NAMAs. Insurance companies have seen their climate, or rather extreme-weather-related, payouts grow over the past 30 years.[6] This is the part of the business that grows alongside the institutional investors' concern for a changing climate. But insurance companies are used to playing more constructive roles in project finance as well, including project finance for climate change related infrastructure investments in renewable energy.

The insurance institutions fall in three categories: the commonly known insurance companies that provide risk insurance for private and corporate legal entities and which are exposed to climate risks due to changing weather patterns and more severe weather events; the Export Credit Agencies (ECAs) that are government supported risk cover institutions offering insurance products that support national export and industry interests, and the reinsurance companies that play decisive roles for front line insurers' provision of risk cover, hence also for climate-related risks.

Private insurance companies provide widely used insurance products for projects and investments that are climate related, particularly in the energy sector – specifically renewable energy. Insurance against technology failure or construction delays provide safety to investors, and are essential for bringing about finance. Insurance is widely used in developed countries, while in NAMA host countries their use mostly depends on developed country technology suppliers bringing them in.

The Export Credit Agencies (ECA) are insurers that provide insurance products with the backing of their national governments, thereby ultimately providing an indirect sovereign risk cover. ECAs are old institutions, the first of which, UK Export Finance (UKEF), was established in the UK in 1921, followed by the Export Credit Fund (EKF) in Denmark in 1922. Others include Hermes (Germany) and EDC (Canada), and, today, virtually all developed countries have one, mostly on the basis of a sovereign guarantee. Most were established as a response to the economic crises after the great wars, filling gaps after capital withdrawals, while in times of growth they fill the gaps that capital and liquidity cannot keep up with.

ECAs are mandated to promote their national interests. Therefore, to avoid competition on a basis of sovereign guarantees, the OECD has established regulations ensuring that all ECAs operate on comparable platforms. Despite their government backing, ECAs operate as private sector insurance entities, providing a range of guarantee products for investments abroad.[7]

The provision of risk guarantees is a necessary instrument to bring in foreign investors in sectors that are particularly dependent on public sector regulation, which, as per the nature of the NAMA, is the case for most. The ECAs are, therefore, crucial if foreign direct investment (FDI) is expected to make up a significant part of the leveraged NAMA financing. While the ECAs are essential for the provision of political risk guaranties for longer term project investments, they also have other products on their shelves that can be activated when engineering the NAMA finance. The ECAs were surprisingly reluctant to move into the climate change market, despite evident market opportunities – particularly in the early 2000s carbon market. Only EKF launched a few carbon market specific insurance products; no one followed suit. The role of the ECAs for the NAMAs is even clearer. Many activities anticipated under NAMAs, mainly infrastructure related, are closer to the core business of the ECAs. The ECAs have the necessary experience in developing and bringing dedicated risk cover products to the market for politically influenced markets and activities. Therefore, they can play a central role in delivering the necessary investor comfort to move NAMAs forward. However, they may find that NAMAs are at least as difficult to grasp as the carbon market was at the beginning of the last decade.

Reinsurance companies pool risks from different insurance companies, and are the first to blow the whistle on unacceptable trends that require payouts. Such trends affect their business. Their reinsurance products that are affected by changing trends in the climate can lead to insurance products being withdrawn from the market. That leaves the risk cover to the insurance companies themselves, with their only response being to increase their premiums or leave the market. The real estate market in Florida, for instance, is at risk of seeing reinsurance companies withdraw, due to risks of rising sea levels. Should that happen, the private insurers may have to follow, or raise premiums dramatically. The importance of reinsurance in bolstering private insurers' appetite for risk cover in less developed markets is obvious, but reinsurance does not change a bad risk into a good one – it is mainly an instrument to spread the good risks. In other words, reinsurance does not reduce the number of defaults and is, therefore, only an instrument to help insurers move into sectors where the perceived risk is higher than the actual risk. 'Trail blazing' risk cover into such areas is a potential role for new climate or NAMA finance.

Hybrid Sources of Financing

Hybrids are another attractive financing source, although they are normally not directly relevant for governments and, therefore, not directly a source for NAMA finance. The hybrids are development institutions that are established with a specific profit objective. Their core capital is public, and devoted to business development objectives in developing countries. The International Finance Corporation (IFC) within the World Bank group is possibly the best known among these institutions, but nearly all developed countries have established such institutions as part of their development assistance activities.[8] Some development banks like the European Bank for Reconstruction and Development (EBRD), Asian Development Bank and African Development Bank have the investment for profit activities embedded within the banks' overall operations as a separate window, or have established dedicated private sector initiatives. The involvement of such hybrid development capital is also a comfort factor for the institutional investor that values the public–private hybrid investors for their built-in risk mitigation qualities, which stem from their identity as bilateral or multilateral donors. While the hybrids cannot guarantee against bad business, despite flawless due diligence, they do pose a *de facto* deterrent against fraudulent behaviour or targeted regulatory harassment.

The hybrids can be actively engaged in discussions of structures that can attract the private sector, as well as – but not necessarily – the foreign direct investor. If the expectation for NAMA financing is a high degree of leveraging of private sector capital, these institutions should, and in fact already do, play significant roles in the future structuring of financing for climate related investment – and thus also in the financial engineering of NAMAs. Together with the ECAs they are clear candidates for taking on the role of aggregators of NAMA finance.

When relevant the hybrids may also engage a structure like the Seed Capital Assistance Facility (SCAF)[9] supported by UNEP and the African and Asian development banks. SCAF is not linked specifically to NAMAs, but instead aims at helping energy investment funds in Asia and Africa, in order to provide seed financing to early stage clean energy enterprises and projects. SCAFs second support line is 'designed to help offset the hurdle of higher perceived risks and lower expected returns when dealing with early stage clean energy project and enterprise developments. … Typically the support is in the range of 10 per cent to 20 per cent of each seed capital investment, paid at the time of investment disbursement.' This resembles hybrid financing, but SCAF does not take any stakes in the projects. The funds are disbursed for costs associated with project documentation, freeing up capital at the investor's end. As such it resembles equity grants (see later).

The philanthropic foundation trustees

Another kind of hybrid is the private philanthropic foundations. These may still be difficult to engage in NAMAs, but the philanthropic landscape is changing, and some foundations are starting to pay attention – if not to the NAMA as a concept, then to their substance. Philanthropic foundations have been in existence, and provided altruistic funding for a multitude of purposes for over a century. Iconic funds such as the Rockefeller Foundation or the Ford Foundation, along with thousands of others, have provided funding for many initiatives that have become institutionalized, or set trends in type or targets of donations. However, most donations are standalone, perhaps not even particularly strategic interventions that reflect the founders' or foundations' specific values. Adding to this the fact that the number of foundations has been growing considerably, counting more than 70,000 in the US alone, it becomes almost impossible to define a strategy for the involvement of philanthropic foundations in the structuring of NAMA financing. However, the language and execution of philanthropy increasingly embrace the principles and concepts of the private sector, as 'the discipline of business thinking appears to enhance the effectiveness of non-governmental organizations and to achieve positive outcomes for communities and society at large' (Rockefeller Philanthropic Advisors, 2008).

The change in approach by some, but certainly not all, trustees favours Mission Related Investment (MRI). This fits particularly well in the financial structures for NAMAs that require the provision of finance that is either more patient, less risk averse, less demanding in terms of return on investment, or generally just more flexible – as long as the promise is a transformational change that, if truly successful and according to plan, will return the investment to the fund. Through this transformation of approach, the philanthropic funds come very close to adopting investment strategies that are akin to the hybrids. The challenge is, however, to make supply and demand meet. Seeking out those foundations that have objectives relevant for a given NAMA, while at the same time adopting a mission related investment programme, could well be a bridge too far.

Philanthropic funds may be the ultimate manifestation of a fragmentation of the financing landscape. It is possibly the one source of funds that is most in need of bridging through an aggregator. Not only are they relatively new in the investment finance picture, but most of them are also relatively small, and, above all, there are many of them. However, their new strategies are at the point of what would be needed to make ends meet in many smaller scale NAMAs, and, therefore, deserve to be specifically addressed, although *not* with the traditional approach of seeking grant financing. Not only is the MRI a decisive move away from this approach, among the trustees themselves, there is no reason to waste philanthropic private sector capital on actions that could have been turned into profitable business.

The Banks

Ultimately, most financial engineering is about reassuring the banks. This is not as unfair as it may sound. In most investments, public as well as private, banks provide the lion's share of the financing. Banks not only provide the largest share of total funding, they do so at the start-up phase, when all forecasts are put to the test. The risk decreases as a project demonstrates its ability to generate cash flow. Banks have a sobering effect in any NAMA discussion, because they are preoccupied with risk – and rightly so, as they do not have any upside on their investments. They only receive interest – no matter how successful the venture they finance, otherwise they receive 'a haircut' if the venture was too much of an adventure. Private investment banks and public development banks play distinct roles, but no matter the pretext they are all risk focused.

Multilateral development banks

The World Bank and the regional development banks have actively embarked on the NAMA agenda. They use their standing and trust funds, put at their disposal by donor countries, to promote the preparation of NAMAs – and they are expected to participate financially in the implementation of NAMAs, by making available the loans that NAMA host countries may need to bring the financing plan together. Their counterparty is the national government, while their hybrid investment arms deal directly with project developers. Their interventions, therefore, will mainly pertain to macro levels and framework conditions for NAMA establishment, or be relevant for large national infrastructure projects, such as hydropower. Smaller scale, project specific interventions mainly succeed through their hybrid private sector arms, as described above, although the previously mentioned Climate Investment

Fund (CIF) may also participate in smaller interventions. The development banks provide financing according to country strategies, with well-established and thorough programming procedures. If the NAMA is high on the political agenda, sooner or later it has to emerge as NAMA priorities in country programming. The development banks have different intervention modalities available depending on the location of the country. Least Developed Countries have access to concessional lending, which is nearly interest free and may have maturities of up to 40 years. Guarantees may be offered occasionally either directly or in the case of the World Bank through MIGA.

National development banks

Most countries have one or more development banks, the purpose of which is to finance central national development projects. Quite often they participate in closed financing arrangements between the publicly owned development bank and a publicly owned utility. In that sense, they are natural partners for most of the larger scale NAMAs, and should be central partners in NAMA development, where they would not only add financial expertise, but also possibly contribute with existing cooperation links to international finance, including the multilateral development banks.

Green Bonds

The green bond (or environmental bond or climate bond) has become an increasingly realistic financing vehicle with significant potentials for bringing in private capital to climate-related investments and, thus, also NAMAs. Its advantage is that it allows particularly institutional investors with no capacity for project specific due diligence processes to deliver their part in the financial engineering of NAMAs. The bond market has become a common way for larger corporation to raise capital in the market without having to go through the stock market. It may become one of the central building blocks for the financing of NAMAs as well, especially if combined with other means and instruments.

The Climate Bonds Initiative put the simple question: if you have a choice between two bonds with the same yield, why would you not buy the one that helps tackle climate change?[10] Surprisingly, there could be many answers to the effect that such new venturing is too exotic. It might embody a higher degree of volatility, risk, impermanence or other problems that a new bond market may face. It is not helpful at all that the carbon market went bust just recently, despite much international political support. It would be naïve to think that this has gone unnoticed and left no traces in the minds of the investors.

It should at least have the green bond issuer consider if the green bond can be left to itself and the market without a dependable safety net. At least its potential could be manifold if properly supported. A first step in this direction was achieved in 2014 when a coalition of 14 major finance institutions joined hands in supporting a set of voluntary guidelines for green bonds to finance environmentally friendly activities,[11] among these importantly guiding the use of proceeds from bond issuance towards, but not limited to:

- Renewable energy
- Energy efficiency (including efficient buildings)
- Sustainable waste management
- Sustainable land use (including sustainable forestry and agriculture)
- Biodiversity conservation
- Clean transportation
- Clean water and/or drinking water

The World Bank and other central issuers of green bonds stand behind the voluntary guidelines.

According to the Climate Bonds Initiative (CBI) there was approximately USD 346 billion in climate-themed bonds at the beginning of 2013 (Climate Bonds Initiative 2013). These are bonds that are labelled 'green' or 'climate' from issuers or projects which are wholly dedicated to climate-related activities. However, the majority of these bonds are issued on the basis of assets in developed countries except, notably, China that represents more than a third. 75 per cent of the bonds are used for the financing of railways arguing a modal shift from air transport.

The first challenge is the geography of the NAMA. The CBI flyer[12] 'Bonds and Climate Change' lists only China, Brazil and South Korea as host countries for climate bonds issuance among developing and transition economies. Bringing the institutional investors on board for developing country assets more generally would likely, at least initially, as a minimum require a reputable issuer such as the World Bank or other development banks – or the involvement of insurers.

A second challenge may be the relatively smaller scale infrastructure in developing countries and therefore smaller investments that may not justify bonds issuance. However, it is conceivable to issue a government green bond in a developing country with significant amounts of bilateral assistance in the state budget. Such government climate bonds could be guaranteed by the ECAs and used for the funding of a portfolio of climate related investments in accordance with the above guideline.

As bond yields fall, and returns on equity investments fall as well, the demand for alternative investments increases. This may help shifting part of the institutional investors' portfolios to higher yielding, less mature markets. The pension funds target up to 10 per cent of investments in new types of assets driven by decreasing bond yields.

Blending

There is every reason to believe that the NAMA developer will lose his way among the financiers, and the different roles they may play – and the products they may offer – for the financial engineering of a NAMA. With no particular skills for interaction with most of these institutions, it is not surprising that the most common inclination is to look for a grant from a bilateral donor organization. A grant can come in late in the process of designing the NAMA – even come in last and, thus, not require any consideration throughout the design process. But grants are few and far between, and grant-based NAMA implementation is not sustainable in the long term and, therefore, fundamentally violates the increasing demand for transformational changes through NAMAs.

There seems to be a thorough miscommunication about the nature of the NAMA – or at least the nature of its financing – if there is any communication at all. Part of the explanation may be that donors are reluctant to be explicit about the conditions for funding, which ultimately will adhere to traditional investment virtues – or the funding will be directed towards familiar preparatory work that brings no asset investments on the ground. Being less clear about it does not help. Being clear about it is not easy either. When the NAMA Facility circulated its draft eligibility criteria for applications under the scheme there was a common dismissal among prospective applicants[13] that no NAMA proponent in the current state of affairs would be able to satisfy the demands conveyed by the draft document. This shortfall of capacity pertains not only to the financial side of the NAMA – but it pertains *also* to the financing.

Building up capacity among NAMA host countries in navigating the international finance sector may not be the most efficient way to bridge the gap. If the financing sector adopts a wait-and-see attitude, the financing 'readiness' may never materialize. One of the instruments thought to be constructive on the supply side is the idea of 'blending'. UNDP is promoting the blending on the recipient's side (UNDP, 2011), which, in effect, is a promotion of the national climate funds that are ready to receive the funds from donors. This is not helpful. It places the burden on the NAMA host countries to figure out how to apply the funding in the most efficient way. Moreover, it perpetuates the perception that NAMA funding consists of grants allocated by donors to national NAMA funds. It isolates the countries from exposure to the 'real' financing market, and it excludes a number of financiers from participating, because the funds approach does not fit their mode of financing.

Blending on the supply side, in the form of an 'aggregator', holds more perspective. The aggregator's role would be to draft a financing model for a given NAMA, and interact with the financing institutions that are offered to play a role in its implementation. Aggregators may be private businesses that offer their services to NAMA host countries, or NAMA developers, or they may be public or publicly supported institutions that fundamentally do the same. The hybrids, as well as the ECAs, have been identified here as very relevant candidates for taking on the job of aggregator. It may even be a role for the GCF. If so, it would need to possess, or build up, a comprehensive network among financiers, but it might not be in a financing role, itself. It may, however, play an active role in the identification of gaps in the financial engineering toolbox, and actively promote their development among the donor community or any of the other types of financiers that could be the most relevant host of such new additions to the toolbox.

Summing Up

NAMA financing is not necessarily in the hands of NAMA finance institutions. Instead, the most important sources of financing are a number of existing financiers with financing instruments that are not dedicated to NAMAs. Among these, hybrid financiers and guarantors, such as the export credit agencies, are likely to play central roles in the future financial engineering of NAMAs – either with their current toolbox or by adding or revising current tools. Among these, enhanced guarantees and green bonds are likely those that can create the largest transformational changes in NAMA financing – the enhanced guarantee because that is the single instrument that can leverage most investments from the private sector, and the green bond mostly due to its prospective enhancement of NAMA host countries' cash flow capacity. The few dedicated NAMA financiers, notably the NAMA Facility, present themselves as financial supermarkets, with a product range that is adaptable to any financing needs – although it could take advantage of more specialized institutions' experience instead.

Chapter 7

ENGINEERING AND
LEVERAGING THE FINANCE

Leveraging and engineering are two sides of the same coin. While leveraging pertains to the raising of capital, the engineering is a plan for deploying it. The more efficient the deployment model, the more likely it is to leverage larger amounts with less seed capital.

Developing a financing model for a NAMA is a process that must be integrated with the NAMA development itself. Further emphasized by the 'official' guidance for NAMA development, the financing model for the NAMA will help shape the NAMA design, determine its implementation modalities and ultimately establish the viability of the proposed action.

The first step is to acknowledge that the basic financing for any NAMA, supported as well as unilateral, will originate in the national – or lower administrative level – budget. NAMAs tend to be revisions of current policies within current budgets, rather than the creation of entirely new ones. Therefore, familiarity with the national budget is crucial to the way in which NAMA financing comes together. The 'official' NAMA guidance is blunt on this message. While this is positive, it may be difficult to find sufficient resonance among policymakers in NAMA host countries. Nevertheless, for the transformational NAMAs envisaged, such budget analysis is crucial.

Current public budget lines contain essential information about present priorities in sectors relevant to emissions reduction, including those pertaining to undesirable conduct in terms of emissions reduction, like fossil fuel subsidies. Analysing the national budget, even at the sector level, may be a challenge, although most administrative bodies would have a relatively good impression of their own sector budget. Potential NAMA developers outside the public administration may have difficulties in getting a precise picture of the sector finances, but when it comes to assessing the current *climate* finance, or the finance related to the subsectors relevant for emissions reduction, even the administration may face a challenge.

To assist in budget analysis in search of public climate expenditure, UNDP and the Overseas Development Institute (ODI) presented the Climate Public

Expenditure and Institutional Review (CPEIR) in 2012. This built on the approaches of recent years to assess public expenditures in developing countries for environmental purposes (PEER) (Swanson and Lunde, 2003; Lawson and Bird, 2008). In addition to providing insights into the current (public) financial flows related to climate change, the CPEIR could have potential as a more generally adoptable starting point for longer term government-led stakeholder dialogues.

A PEER study in Bhutan in 2011, by Rinzin and Linddal, reconstructed the national budget to explore environmental spending, and identified 4,600 relevant expenditure lines – 400 of which accounted for approximately 80 per cent of the environmental public expenditure. Capital expenditure also constituted 80 per cent of the total, whereas local government accounted for about a third of the expenditure. Both of these issues – the balance between capital and recurrent spending, and between central government and local expenditure – must be addressed when examining climate change related expenditure.

PEER and CPEIR offer guidance on how public expenditure on climate change actions can be examined on the three dimensions of policy, institutional and budgetary analysis (UNDP/ODI 2012). The CPEIR analysis aims at:

- Securing a better understanding of the formulation of climate change policy and its linkages to expenditure through national strategies and action plans;
- Improving the understanding of the role and responsibilities of institutions involved in managing the response to climate change and their interaction; and
- Quantifying climate change related expenditures in the national budget, and through other funding channels.

Just as there is no international definition of climate finance, so there is no internationally recognized definition of climate expenditure and therefore no clear boundaries of such spending. It must include budget allocations for both mitigation and adaptation, although in the context of NAMAs only mitigation related budget elements are relevant, and it should describe the balance between capital and recurrent spending, and between central government and local expenditure. In particular the role played by the Ministry of Finance is central in responding to climate change in light of potential new flows of climate finance becoming available through enhanced international support. Local government institutions and the administrative mandates delegated to the sub-national level are also central in the analysis of institutions responsible for implementing the budget. Finally, but equally important, are the roles played by the profit and non-profit sectors, which in many countries are essential implementers of climate change policies and practices. Their motivations need to be understood, and their structures and capacity limitations taken into account when looking at budgeting and re-budgeting for the improved effectiveness of available public finance. Obviously it is in this context that environmental fiscal reform must be considered.

When examining the current institutional structure of the budget the motivations behind the structure should also be considered, as they may represent barriers that could be difficult to overcome. For instance, the most pertinent emissions reduction options exist in the strategic energy sector where ownership structures may be more of a political consideration than an economic one. For a number of reasons, political, independent power producers (IPPs) do not always have access. Corporatizing the domestic infrastructure and leaving it in control of national interests is common, but opening it to Foreign Direct Investment (FDI) is often a mixed blessing. While it holds the potential to create economic growth by generating jobs, to many it resembles 'selling the family silver'. Private sector involvement is, therefore, not always the answer to leveraging additional climate finance through NAMA design – or alternative models for its involvement must be devised.

Transformation

There are two fundamental interests expressed by the donor community: 1) interventions must have a permanent effect, being 'transformational' in nature; 2) interventions must leverage the largest possible proportion of finance, outside the NAMA finance sphere. Permanence is favoured not only by donors that are emphasizing the transformational character of interventions, but also by the private sector, which favours stable and predictable investment environments and conditions. The more permanent and trustworthy the investment environment, the greater is the interest in it and, thus, the better the chance of mobilizing investment capital. The two interests – transformation and leveraging – are mutually supporting objectives.

The cash flows in a sector, established through instruments deployed by the public sector, determine the values and preferences among the stakeholders in the sector. Changing those preferences on a permanent basis is the essence of a transformational change. Therefore, 'transformation' has to do with a change of financial flows. Implicitly, the financial engineering of NAMAs is also about altering the financial flows in a sector. Thus, there is an intricate link between the transformational character of a NAMA, and the degree to which it permanently alters current financial flows – in a way that ultimately reduces the emission externality pertaining to that particular activity.

There is a parallel in financing to the 'non-transformational' NAMA. Cash flows reflect processes, characterizing the operation of a system. Standalone investments do not. Financing a single project is in a sense static. The system remains. There is no transformation – unless the single project is of a scale that has transformational character, for instance the establishment of a waste incineration plant for the capital of Egypt, which is being considered. Otherwise, transformation is more likely to be a result of a permanent change in the cash flows and thus a permanent change in the resulting incentives and disincentives. For example, adding a single wind farm to a carbon intensive energy system, based on an individual power purchase agreement, is not transformational. Establishing a feed-in tariff system that allows the private sector to invest in renewable energy in anticipation of stable returns is.

Clearly, such definitions cannot be black or white and render activities either transformational or non-transformational. For instance, the privatization of public infrastructure may transform the sector. It could be turned into a NAMA by adding emissions reduction objectives to the list of performance requirements in a tendering procedure, possibly as an evaluation criterion for the bidding on a fixed fee public service concession, awarded to the bidder offering the largest emissions reduction over a given period.

Assessing such investment options, the private investor considers that projects in different sectors have varying risk profiles. The privatization of existing infrastructure with a known history and position in the market has a more easily predictable risk profile, and is, therefore, easier to finance than a greenfield project. It may also be easier to attract commercial debt for energy supply projects than for road projects, for example, because traffic forecasting is more difficult than predictions of power consumption. Other sectors will have forecasts that are more or less predictable. The bottom line is that the better the foundation for the prediction of the infrastructure service demand, the 'safer' the cash flow prediction and, thus, the safer the debt service – which ultimately is a comfort for the banks.

Leveraging Finance from Different Sources

The above seems to indicate that the ultimate objective for all NAMA financing is to bring the private sector, and its banking partners, on board at any price. While this is not the case, the discourse among the developed countries, in particular, is that the leveraging of private sector financing is paramount, if the USD 100 billion mark is to be reached. But there are certain unavoidable dynamics that have been missed in that statement. Only few still expect the GCF to become a large concentration of capital for deployment in investment objects. Rather, the GCF will consist of a small real money injection capacity and a much larger virtual financial leveraging capacity, employing all existing delivery systems for funding, as described in the previous chapter. While some may find this disappointing, it is in fact good. If the entire funding stemmed from a single source, essential checks and balances in the finance markets would be lost, investment criteria and decision parameters would become monolithic, and administrative routines would bury capital flows under the weight of bureaucracy.

'Leveraging' is the preferred term for describing that much of the funding has to originate from other sources. The less cash injected into the Fund, the higher the leveraging has to be. A general principle, from a leveraging point of view, is that the leveraging model must be completed before the instrument or initiative is launched. Small-scale demonstrations may be tried out with national funding only, but otherwise sufficient funding should be secured before launch, to avoid the risk of having to change mid-way. Discontinuity and small scale are significant deterrents to private sector involvement.

The 'who goes first' dilemma

The term 'leveraging' is also used in the CDM to explain how much the carbon revenues produced by the emissions reduction has generated, or leveraged, in terms of investment capital. This calculation is very complex because it depends greatly on the valuation of the carbon asset and the number of years over which it is seen. However, it is not uncommon to see leveraging values of 20 to 30 times, meaning that the carbon asset has created investments 20 to 30 times higher than its own value. Oddly, in the CDM, leveraging works the other way around. The more capital has been leveraged (for a given amount of emissions reduction), the more expensive the emissions reduction – contrary to the objective of cost efficient emissions reduction. So while a high degree of leveraging in the CDM is 'bad' – contrary to what is normally thought – a high degree of leveraging for NAMA financing is 'good', from the perspective that it signals that little effort has been required to activate other sources of financing, which are normally attracted only by profitability motives. The reason for the difference, of course, is that it is not the same parameters that are measured. In the CDM, it is the value of the product, the emissions reduction that is compared to the amount of finance needed to produce it. In NAMAs, the measurement of leveraging only – and correctly – looks at the leveraging of finance, in accordance with the statement that cost inefficient emissions reduction is not an investment deterrent.

Leveraging is a discipline that involves a financier in a leading role, driven by a certain purpose or strategy, the reach and effect of which

Figure 11. The right order of leveraging

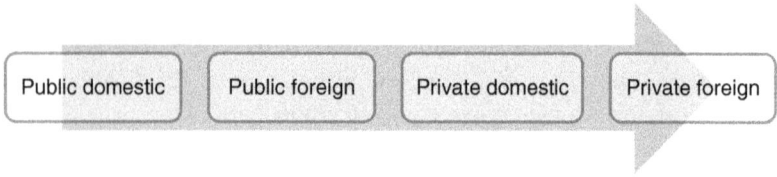

ideally is proportionate to his leveraging capability. In private financing, 'who goes first' is relatively straightforward. It involves the origination of equity – the founding capital for an activity. The equity investor, however, is not the one who takes the first step in the financial engineering of a NAMA. They only enter when the public sector has done its homework. The first mover is, inevitably, the national public sector – the regulator that wishes for a transformational change in his sector, and starts looking at the current cash flows in the sector with the objective of identifying the specific barriers for changing the financial flows towards promoting the lower emission pathway.

The domestic public institution that intends to develop a NAMA may be in one of two situations: 1) either it has a budget to initiate a leveraging exercise; or 2) it does not. Having a budget that can be brought into play is of course the best starting point. This does not have to be a free budget allocation; most likely it will be the budget currently used for an activity or service in a sector that entails the emission of greenhouse gases – e.g., energy, transport, agriculture or construction. If the available finance is insufficient for the intended initiative, there are four general directions to go for additional funding, as established in Chapter 4: domestic-public, domestic-private, international-public and international-private.

Additional domestic public funding

As already established, the point of departure for leveraging funds for NAMA implementation is the current national budget. The PEER and CPEIR instruments may have identified the current expenditures in the national budget that could be relevant cash flows and investments to incorporate in the NAMA, but they do not provide any guidance on how to initiate any reallocation.

Environmental Fiscal Reform is the discipline to engage in. A reallocation of funds within the promoting line ministry's own sector is the traditional first alternative. Less popular, presumably, would be attempts of cannibalizing other line ministries' budgets. More visionary ways of looking at it were suggested through the EFR exploiting that initiatives in one sector may reduce costs in another. The possible savings in the health sector from improvements in the surrounding environment are normally very difficult to quantify, because savings typically occur years later with uncertain causality. Cross-subsidizing options would need to have costs and benefits occur at about the same time. For instance a solar PV programme in a rural area fully dependent on subsidized fossil fuel would have savings on subsidies occur at about the same time as the investments in solar PV sets. However, even with such a beneficial starting point, moving the subsidy budget into a solar PV purchase programme would probably not be straightforward.

Some countries are finding ways in which domestic funding originating from savings or revenues in one activity can be activated for the funding of another activity regardless of its sector affiliation. As mentioned, Mexico intends to establish a NAMA Fund that can accrue such amounts and at the same time serve as a national coordinator for NAMA financing – including international funding. Such structures require a general national priority for NAMA development, and the awareness that without activating the possible national funding sources, e.g., through savings on subsidies as above, the chances of attracting other substantial funding – private or public – are slim.

One of the major challenges to the activation of the national budget, as the starting point for leveraging funds from other sources, is that the NAMA development is commonly anchored in the Ministry of Environment. The anchoring seems intuitively logical. The national focal points for communication with the UNFCCC Secretariat on NAMAs, the National Designated Entities (NDEs), are situated – with very few exemptions – in the national Ministry of Environment. Together with the national Ministry of Foreign Affairs, the national Ministry of Environment is commonly responsible for climate change negotiations, dividing the responsibilities among themselves along political and technical lines.

This make-up of negotiation delegations entails natural limitations in such substances as overall policy strategy and national budgets – subjects that were of little consequence for the implementation of the CDM, but which are central to the NAMA. While the CDMs were targeting isolated private sector project activities within existing policy frameworks, the typical NAMA is about altering policy frameworks towards less emission intensive development.

The Ministry of Environment is typically a weak ministry, with little influence on national politics and few emissions falling within its sphere of responsibility. Nearly all national emissions fall in other sectors: energy, industry, transport and agriculture. Only waste, water, and waste water are significant contributors to emissions, and are typically the responsibility of the Ministry of Environment. Hence, the interesting budgets are initially beyond reach, and the Ministry of Environment may instead be tempted to try raising all the NAMA financing from international sources, without any contribution from the national budget. That is ill advised. Bringing the line ministry of the sector of interest on board is a minimum – transformative NAMAs, however, would be somewhat unimaginable without the Ministry of Finance on board.

Approaching international financiers

Demonstrating the ability to mobilize national resources, either through government budgets or, alternatively, by demonstrating a willingness to regulate the private sector (see following section) is a good starting point for approaching international financiers. Chapters 5 and 6 presented the diverse institutions with an equally diverse set of financing instruments at their disposal. They have their distinct mandates, preferences and modes of operation. Currently, a few of them prefer NAMA related activities, but, generally, most of them are welcoming investments or finance options that comply with traditional virtues – such as political support, stakeholder acceptance, low risk, high impact and profitability, no matter their label. It is imaginable that the GCF, once operational, may impact the bilateral donor landscape. Some will pull out of direct involvement, while others might engage in models that are linked with the GCF. Those that invest together with the private sector will continue to go their own way. One thing unites them: they all need to demonstrate that their money is well spent.

For some, but not all, NAMA financiers, that means that the activity leads to emissions reduction. As already mentioned the 'official' NAMA guidance emphasizes that, more often than not, emissions reduction is the co-benefit of other more important investment motivations. The NAMA financier, however, may still wish to have the initiative packaged as emissions reduction with a budget and an estimate of the anticipated impact. The budget is not necessarily the cost. It may be that the target of the NAMA is the investment in energy infrastructure worth several hundred millions of dollars. The objective of the financial engineering of the NAMA is to establish new cash flows in a transformational change of the sector that will ultimately result in these investments, and not to deliver the financing of the infrastructure. Therefore, in a presentation to a potential NAMA financier, a more general provision of economic data and a flexibility in revising the current financial flows in the sector is more valuable, and allows the financier or donor to participate in the financial engineering of the NAMA. This may result in a lower budget, and, therefore, a lower cost per tonne of greenhouse gas emissions reduced.

Donors that are grant-based normally do not engage in implementation, but only in different forms of preparation – e.g., technical assistance, capacity building, sector strategies and other activities that are not related to physical assets. In that respect, the NAMAs may have an advantage over earlier emissions reduction initiatives, since most NAMAs are policy related. Hence, the cost of formulating a policy that promotes the reduction of emissions, a regulation that drives investment into cleantech, or a programme for rural electrification is perfectly in line with traditional donor intervention. Where an intervention does not require a national budget, but only a will to regulate and possibly impose investments in the private sector, donor grant financing may entertain the cost of devising regulations that most efficiently achieve the desired results. The next step – e.g., the provision of funding for an enhancement of cash flow – is where the donor organization will feel challenged. This is where the financial engineering of the NAMA will have to stand the test. If it works well, the physical assets will be financed through a number of instruments, activated by the private sector and its banking partners – if private sector involvement is the ultimate objective.

This has implications for the many possibilities of foreign donor intervention. The donors need to realize that their traditional model of intervention – grant financing of technical assistance – needs to be added another gear. While the development of policies and regulations that can help change cash flows in a sector may well be compatible with the traditional donor intervention, the financing model for additional cash flows is not. A constant provision of a monthly grant, over 10 or 20 years, is not a viable option. As such, other models need to be visualized. Knowing the shortcomings of current donor funding is useful, but it may also be a hindrance if unchallenged during the financial engineering of a NAMA.

Country experience or existing assistance programming of a donor in a country is another important criterion for donor involvement. Assistance is not spread over a large number of countries, but concentrated on a smaller number – particularly for smaller donors. It is, therefore, a puzzle, which the national Ministry of Finance can help clear up, to identify which donors are already active in a given developing country and in what particular economic sectors.

Engaging the local private sector

The CDM experience is merciless. Despite intentions to foster billions of investment dollars flowing from foreign sources into CDM host countries, investments never came as the CDM never managed to change the investment fundamentals that kept the foreign investor away. The CDM ultimately thrived on the local investor. Private business, foreign and local alike, is preoccupied with core business and core competencies (Prahalad, Hamel, 1990). Corporations do not invest in all profitable investment options they come across and do not venture out of their core business easily. In addition, other issues have undeterminable influence on investment decisions. Corporate management makes investment decisions while relying on intuition, employing moral values, personal convictions and perceptions, individual assessments, and corporate 'truths'. They focus on their core competencies, and are constrained by the scarcity of resources and information. Only a part of these elements can be attributed an economic value, objectively. It is important to note that if a potential investment does not pass the 'strategy test', it is not likely to even reach the level of calculation. For this reason, industrial energy efficiency has a very hard time finding priority in industry. Devoting capital to non-core business at the expense of investing in expanding its core business base, leaves the company more vulnerable to competition, which is potentially life threatening. Missing an emissions reduction option is not – not even a profitable one.

However, the government can impose such gold picking by regulation, although it must be imposed evenly in order to not disturb competition in the market. Such disturbances could have unwanted consequences – potentially even shifting the balance in favour of foreign competition that will not be under the same restriction.

Regulation is commonplace. That is what government is. The private sector is used to regulation, and contrary to expectation is not against it, as long as it is predictable, indiscriminating, and does not significantly erode competitiveness. Particularly in sectors where investment horizons are very long, like the energy sector, predictability of regulatory regimes is crucial. If regulation is not in conformity with these three requirements, the private sector will try to circumvent – especially if they know that enforcement is rudimentary.

Nevertheless, regulation is a good way to activate, in particular, the profitable emissions reduction options like energy efficiency. Being required, by law, to devote investment capital to profitable investments is less of a burden than being required to invest in unprofitable ones. Regulation that requires unprofitable investments may be softened through a parallel provision of a funding model, possibly incorporating bank financing against a government guarantee. The private sector entity would take a loan, low interest because of the guarantee, to finance the investment and repay the loan over a period to ease the pain. While the guarantee is not free, and may marginally influence the credit standing of the country (although that would demand a sizeable guarantee scheme) it does not require any immediate cash.

The private sector may also encompass corporatized public entities. These are common in the energy sector. Such corporations should in principle be regarded as private organizations with private sector investment motives and drivers. Government ownership may facilitate the alignment of development strategies, but the most important feature of the structure is an easier or cheaper access to capital – also through the international markets.

The private sector is not only companies, but also citizens. The above is just as applicable to households as it is to companies. The CDM Programmes of Activity have been instrumental in providing examples on how to distribute large quantities of household installations based on different models for channelling carbon revenues into the initiatives. Such initiatives can also be undertaken as NAMAs, although a coexistence of the NAMA and the PoA was rendered problematic in Chapter 2.

Other examples for engaging household – or corporate – financing has been the introduction of smart meters in some developed countries, allowing households to produce their own electricity and have their meters running 'backwards'. Although these investments are relatively more expensive per installed megawatt than larger scale central installations, these initiatives have the private households overtaking the investment responsibility, typically in a home micro wind turbine or a small solar PV installation. But where energy taxes are charged, the government loses revenues when people produce their own power. This, however, is rarely the case in NAMA host countries, where fuel subsidies remain widespread – and the existence of subsidies, instead, is detrimental to the involvement of private finance.

Attracting Foreign Direct Investment (FDI)

Foreign direct investors are selective. The model adopted by the CDM, for instance, made no impression on them. The CDM did not create the transformational change that should have altered the perception of investment conditions. Investment climates cannot be changed overnight by the introduction of a new mechanism. Investors look at country risk; guarantors look at country risk too, and country risk is determined, among other things, by the regulator's attitude and past moves. When investing, the private investor typically takes out an investment guarantee in an Export Credit Agency (ECA, see Chapter 6), which charges not only according to the project specific risks, but also following the OECD-based classification of the country. The riskier the investment and investment destination, the higher the price for risk cover.

Some developing countries, mainly Least Developed Countries, do not even have a risk rating. This virtually renders FDI almost impossible.

A high risk classification is not only an indication of the risk level, it is also a direct cost that means that in risky countries, the return on investment must be that much higher. Figure 10 illustrated the costs affiliated with risk. Foreign investors – and, sometimes, domestic investors, as well – will easily require 30 per cent or more in return on equity. This is intuitively unfair to the observer – the poorest countries have to pay the highest price for the services – but it is a logic-based conclusion and a vicious circle that is hard to change. The required return on investment can be tempered by establishing comfort factors that reduce risk. Sovereign guarantees are an option, though the solidity of the regulator is reflected in the risk categorization. A sovereign guarantee provided by a country in which a considerable share of the state budget is donor funds, is either a developed country guarantee, by proxy, or a very uncertain guarantee. Therefore, investors may want to adopt another strategy, such as investing together with a reputed investor like the World Bank or a foreign development finance institution. The hybrids are usually a good and flexible investment partner, but even those are not insensitive to risk, and will often require the involvement of ECAs. Ensuring the mobility of assets (for instance, some power plants are built on barges) can be an extreme, but very efficient, way of securing the asset.

The foreign investor has the whole world as potential for deployment of investment capital, and unless there are very good reasons to invest in country X, they may shift their interest to country Y. The investment drivers must be found in the core business of the private investors that a country wants to attract. It may open its transport business by offering free concessions to BRT (Bus Rapid Transit) operators – which may not be a persuasive business proposition in many places – or award BOT contracts for grid connected wind projects, which is only attractive if it is supported by a risk-free long-term feed-in tariff. It may allow ESCOs (Energy Service Companies) to provide efficiency services to state-owned enterprises, or invite investors to grow energy crops for export on waste lands. There are many options, and those mentioned here are not chosen for their appeal – only to illustrate that while it does not have to be particularly beautiful, it does have to be profitable.

The Right Order of Leveraging

Understanding the dynamics behind these four sources of financing is the first step towards the engineering of the finance. Orchestrating the instruments available is the second. Identifying where and how international donor funding can be injected most efficiently in the financing model, is the third and final step.

The logic in the right order of leveraging is that the national public sector must go first. National priority, support, and willingness to transformation is imperative in order to inspire not only a national private sector, but also the international donor community, and ultimately foreign investment. The NAMA host country's private sector will rarely have any leveraging power over the foreign public donor. Instead, initial national funding, possibly provided through a redirection of existing financial flows in the sector of the proposed NAMA, should be instrumental in leveraging international donor funding. These two sources, combined, have a better chance of orchestrating a suite of instruments that can inspire national private investment and, if successful, possibly the international private investor as well.

Here is an understandable challenge: the current rhetoric surrounding the USD 100 billion in developed countries' annual support for climate action in developing countries is that the private sector will have to contribute significantly – perhaps as much as 80 per cent. This may not be the preferred outcome from the perspective of the NAMA host countries, but even more troubling is that before the international private sector is likely to put its investment capital at work, the NAMA host countries' private sectors will have had to take the first steps – as they did in the CDM. Developed country support will, therefore, have to be targeted more at leveraging the NAMA host countries' private sector financing capacity, and less at leveraging their own private sector investments.

UNEP FI and IISD's (UNEP FI/IISD, 2013) study of developing countries' climate finance capacity is very relevant, and underscores that in the CDM, the CER generation capacity is limited, first and foremost, by developing countries' unilateral investment capacity (Lütken and Michaelowa, 2008). This conclusion was based on earlier research (Lütken, 2005) that estimated this capacity at USD 140 billion per year for renewable energy, energy efficiency, and waste-related investments. Incidentally, this corresponds well with the investments actually recorded under the CDM, raising the obvious question of whether investment capacity in NAMA host countries is already exhausted. It is not.

The premise for this calculation is a historical distribution between traditional energy investments and the emission friendly alternatives. According to the same calculations, the USD 140 billion corresponds only to about 8 per cent of the total relevant investments, leaving 92 per cent open to a revision of investment priorities – first and foremost those investments that go into fossil-fuel-based energy generation. This is the prime, though not the only, target for the leveraging exercise.

Figure 12. The financing value chain

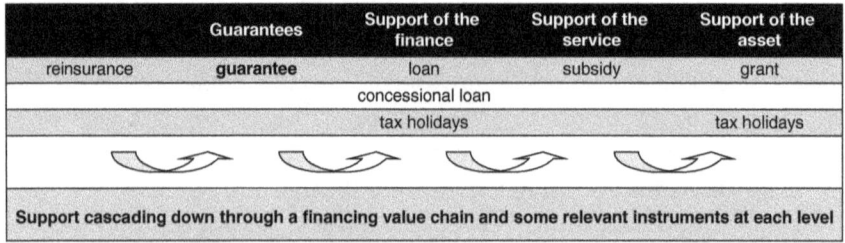

	Guarantees	Support of the finance	Support of the service	Support of the asset
reinsurance	**guarantee**	loan	subsidy	grant
		concessional loan		
		tax holidays		tax holidays

Support cascading down through a financing value chain and some relevant instruments at each level

While there is a right order of leveraging among the four different sources of financing there is also a right order of leveraging the types of financing in relation to assets. Figure 12 illustrates the relationship between them. At the same time it represents a financing value chain, which may be combined with the instruments that a NAMA host country regulator has at his disposal – according to Figure 8.

Having mapped the national budget's relevant cash flows, their size and direction, a well as the investment budgets lays the foundation for a determination of the optimal type of intervention. If support is needed to permanently change these cash flows – or the investment priorities – the injection of support is not equally efficient in all four streams. The financing value chain helps illustrate the relation between the different forms of financial instruments. Moreover, these are the options for deployment of public sector funds, including donor funds, and thus implicitly the leveraging instruments. The structuring of these, employing different sources of public funding, will ultimately determine the financial contribution from other sources, notably the private sector.

The intervention options from Figure 8 are distributed in the four categories in Figure 12. The arrows indicate their mutual relationship. Provision of guarantees reduces the cost of financing; concessional loans reduce the cost of acquiring the asset; support of the service increases the return on the investment; a grant for the asset naturally reduces the cost of implementation.

Moving further up this already existing leveraging chain and having the leveraging effect 'cascading' down through an existing system is probably the most efficient way of applying NAMA finance with the purpose of leveraging other financing sources. Supporting an already established support system such as the current export credit system's guarantees is likely to have much further reaching effects than for instance providing a grant for a physical asset based on an incremental cost calculation, which in this model is the least efficient – and unfortunately the often chosen – mode of intervention.

Figure 13 is an even more expanded illustration of the financing value chain, incorporating the financing instruments and financiers described in Chapter 5 and 6 – as well as a few instruments that are suggested in the following chapter. The figure combines the right order of leveraging; the logic in the

Figure 13. Instruments in the financing value chain

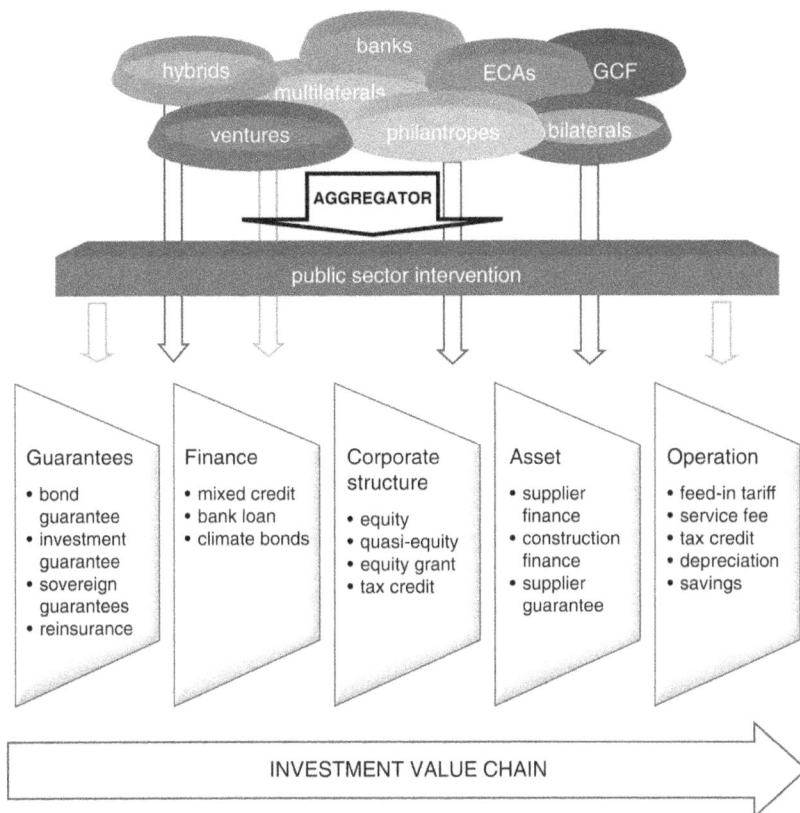

financing value chain; the relevant financing institutions, and the deployment instruments available to the NAMA host country regulator. Combined, it represents a practically endless array of opportunities for putting together a financing plan. While some of these elements are easily applicable in principle, the practical application is complicated by the fact that it will only rarely be done by applying just one instrument. The most efficient model may rest on the injection of grant elements at several places in the structure – which may be a task rather for an aggregator, together with the NAMA host country's Ministry of Finance, than the Ministry of Environment. Even if the optimal instruments can be identified or devised the possible sources of their funding presents another level of complication. An aggregator would be useful and is injected in Figure 13 between the financing institutions and the NAMA host country regulator. The aggregator intervenes as an advisor on the financial engineering of the NAMA and acts as the linkage to the potential sources

Figure 14. Maximizing leveraging

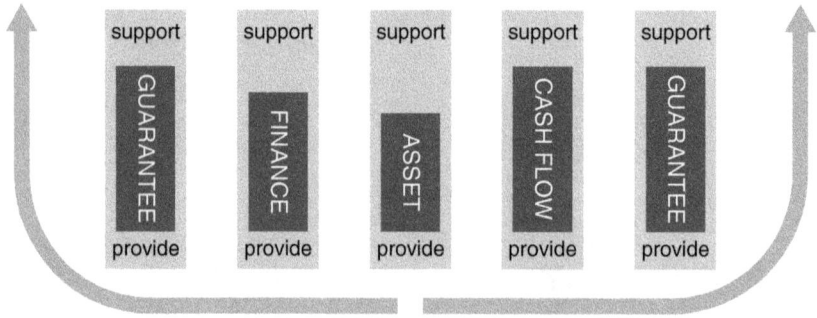

of finance distributed on the types of intervention. More on aggregation in Chapters 8 and 9.

As already indicated the mileage of one dollar of NAMA finance is influenced by the way in which it is spent. The financing value chain illustrated in Figure 14 advocates that NAMA financing intervenes as far back in the financing value chain as possible through the existing public sector delivery system, following the arrows in the figure. This means that the least attractive option in terms of leveraging is to provide a grant for asset investment, only surpassed by supplying the asset in full. Thus differentiation is also made between full provision ('provide') and only supporting ('support') the provision of the financial product. Obviously, the most efficient intervention is suggested to be the support of the existing guarantee system.

It would be conceivable that with this array of options, the financial engineering of NAMAs would mostly be about deciding which instruments are more suitable in a given situation. Unfortunately, that is not the case. In fact, some of the most efficient instruments are not in the toolboxes at all.

With the exception of the CDM no instruments are or have been targeted at the provision of long-term cash flows. Such instruments are incompatible with the way traditional donor funding is allocated. Still, one of the main criteria for the transformational changes sought in NAMAs is that incentives structures in a given sector are altered towards a preference for more desirable investment alternatives – and this requires a permanent change of the cash flows. While the CDM was designed to provide such cash flows, two flaws in its design meant that the cash flow could not be insured in the market and, hence, could not serve as collateral for raising investment capital. Hence the suggestion (in Chapter 3) to reversely engineer the CDM.

The prospective 'new market mechanisms' may reinvent the credit for domestic purposes where national emission trading schemes are one way of establishing long-term cash flows. If safeguards are put in place to prevent market collapses, and the cash flows with sufficient levels of certainty, finance may be engineered around such cash flows. Insurance products addressing non-delivery of, as well as non-payment for, carbon credits would be natural additions to be offered by insurers or possibly donor funds-based guarantee schemes, but otherwise composed of purely domestic private cash flows.

However, in the current absence of such national carbon markets, there is an understandable 'NAMA financing gap'. The current models for applying development and climate assistance are either:

1) Long-term asset financing; or
2) Short-term operational budgets (short grant programmes).

Long-term financing models or platforms for altered and often increased cash flows do not exist among the international financing institutions. Whether the allocation models for development and climate assistance in developed countries can be altered is doubtful. If not, models are needed that can transform short-term operational budgets and long-term asset financing through concessional loans into long-term operational budgets. Also in that respect, the guarantees have something to offer, although they cannot fill the gap completely. The grant financing from donors targeted at NAMA financing must focus on instruments that can leverage cash flows outside the NAMA financing structure, and over and above the reprioritizating of national operational budgets this may well be achieved through improved access to guarantees.

Summing Up

The purpose of NAMA financing is to leverage other sources of funds – the least input for as much output as possible. The extreme case is hard regulation that requires no financing on the part of the NAMA host country regulator, but imposes investments on the part of the regulated. Other instruments are more or less efficient in leveraging mainstream financing. These instruments are relevant at different levels in a financing value chain, where guarantees are at the highest level. It takes little input in the form of a guarantee to leverage significant investment, with the leveraging effect cascading down through the financing value chain through support of the cash flow, support of the finance and the least efficient support for the asset. Hence, only in exceptional cases should investment grant support be provided. Instead, the most important target for increasing the leveraging options for NAMA finance is to concentrate efforts on the insurance system, possibly including reinsurance, analysing the current shortcomings – as CPI has done and as the following chapter will do at length – because that is where the USD 100 billion will have, by far, the largest impact.

Part II

WHAT OUGHT TO BE

Chapter 8

CHALLENGES TO NAMA FINANCE – MANDATES, AGGREGATION AND LACK OF INSTRUMENTS

When looking to finance a NAMA, the identification of the financing value chain is the starting point. Having established the chain, the exercise must focus on identifying options for intervention, as far back in the value chain as possible. That means following the arrows in Figure 14, moving away from the centre and the support of the asset, towards the guarantee that supports the cash flow, which, in turn, supports the loan that supports the asset. Moreover, there is also a differentiation between the provision of a financial instrument (or in extreme cases, the provision of the asset) and the support of an existing one – hence, there is another movement from the bottom to the top in Figure 14.

Following this logic, it is clear that the immediate interest should concentrate on the guarantees, and the institutions that provide them. Guaranties are at the core of any project investment – climate related, or otherwise. The Export Credit Agencies (ECAs) already play an important role, bringing about the financing for projects that would otherwise not materialize. The ECAs are a natural place to look for enhanced risk coverage, either from existing guarantees of products or possibly through expansion of coverage – within the limitations dictated by the OECD rules, or potentially by calling for a loosening of these rules. These rules are not easily changed, however. They are 'consensus rules', or 'gentlemen's agreements', that ensure that all ECAs operate on the same basis, offer the same type of basic products, and assess (country) risks in a uniform manner. Changing the rules requires a unanimous agreement. While there are other shortcomings in the ECA system, in order to respond to market needs, the more fundamental challenge are the mandates that govern the ECAs – and many other institutions with them, including the donor institutions. Mandates are discussed later in this chapter.

It is a fundamental task and a common approach in policy development advice to identify the barriers that prevent desirable things from happening and the financing from flowing. A common, but very simplistic, barrier is a high up-front cost – the price of the asset – and the immediate temptation to reduce the price of the asset through a grant. According to Figure 14, this is the least efficient way to apply the financing. Furthermore, it has no transformational qualities either. However, the more prevalent barrier is the absence of other financing instruments, leaving an asset grant as practically the only available option.

Few NAMA hosts will be able to draft the requirements for an efficient financing instrument that is currently not being offered in the market, and most will be tempted to go with the traditional model. Resignation on both sides – the typical NAMA developer in the host country's Ministry of Environment, and the majority of the donor community, due to constraints in their mandates – may hinder the development of the right instruments. Before discussing further shortcomings in the financing system, it is worth reverting to the aggregator.

The Aggregation Gap

While the climate change agenda is perhaps not performing worse than other agendas, it is evident that communication across stakeholder groups is less than optimal. The disconnect between the policy level, the funding institutions, and the private sector has observers talking about silos. Despite continuous talk about donor coordination, the government donors and financiers are not shying away from establishing competition among themselves or repeating each other's efforts, in order to respond to their own development strategies. A function that can aggregate financing from different sources and takes it upon itself to promote and support communication across silos would be beneficial under all circumstances, and would bring additional value to the provision of coordination, identification of financing instruments and partners, and would even help identify gaps in the financing landscape for NAMAs.

The fundamental challenge is that there *is* no aggregator, and that in traditional assistance this function has mainly been established on the supply side as donor coordination meetings, when programmes are being implemented – and less so when the programmes are designed. On the demand side, it has been established in the form of budget support or pool funding, where a rapidly decreasing number of donors contribute to one common generic budget instrument. The perspectives for the financial engineering of NAMAs, however, lie in an actively concerted effort to put instruments together in a leveraging exercise. It is a function that has little, if any, experience in the financing community. The aggregator would need to devise a strategy for leveraging finance from the four sources (public/ private, national/international) divided among a multitude of institutions, presented in Chapter 6. Their role is a significant expansion of the one filled by syndicators that were instrumental in the financial engineering of private infrastructure during the 1990s – securitization models in each case arranged by a leading financier. Syndication has been nearly eliminated by the current financial crisis. While the syndicator was organizing several financing sources, in order to bring about financial close for a single project structure, the aggregator must, in addition to that, help structure demands for financing instruments, prospectively deployed through public–public partnerships, that can be presented to the donor community, including the Green Climate Fund.

The idea of formalized aggregators that devise financing models for NAMAs, including proposals for financing instruments, is not straightforwardly implemented, because it interferes with the way in which development assistance is normally deployed. However, keeping in mind that the NAMA funding must be additional, a departure from the traditional deployment model could be considered, for once, by adopting a change in the financing approach. The NAMA Facility has already indicated that is it willing to provide instruments as necessary. That remains to be seen. Otherwise, as the few new NAMA financing sources listed in the NAMA Registry illustrate, NAMA financing schemes do not provide new models of financing. Instead, they produce new selection criteria for provision of traditional (and already existing) financing. They require applicants to describe their ideas and budget before any financing model has been considered that will facilitate such budgeting. Applicants, therefore, at best, may be able to calculate basic 'incremental costs' without any sophistication, which inevitably leads them towards the least efficient NAMA financing model.

It is by no means too late. NAMA financing is in its infancy. Aggregating the finance and devoting different sources to differing purposes can also be done on a case-by-case basis, by shifting teams of financial engineers (for lack of a better title). Whatever the composition of these teams – ad hoc groups of representatives from different financing institutions assisted by financial engineers or a formalized aggregating company or institution with the task to put together the best possible financing structure for a given NAMA – they would have to follow a strategy that brings as much existing investment capital into service of the climate change mitigation objective as possible. The degree of leveraging involved in reaching the Green Climate Fund's goal of USD 100 billion per year of climate finance remains a subject of debate. However, the discussion is rather fruitless. The degree of leveraging is determined on a case-by-case basis, depending on the subject of finance. Leveraging is not a goal in itself; it is a means to achieving an

Figure 15. The aggregators' central role in organizing financing

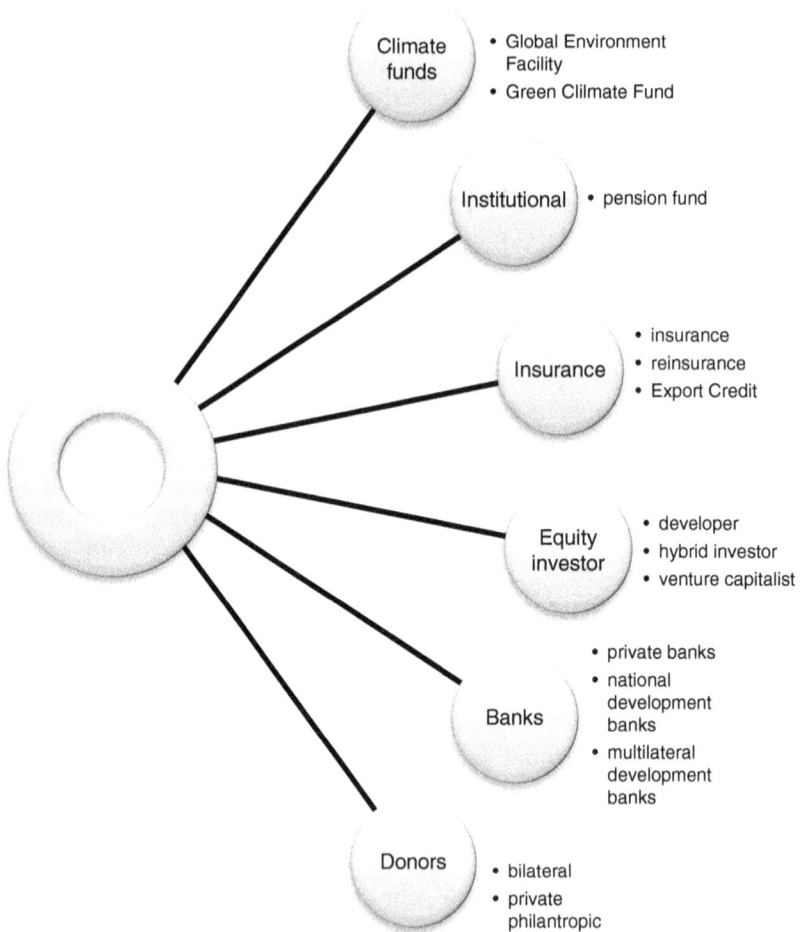

end, which is nationally appropriate. It may well be that the requirements for modifications and alterations to a given project or policy, from different sources of leveraged financing, will divert the implementation modalities of the NAMA so far away from the original intentions that the action is no longer nationally appropriate. At this point, of course, leveraging has gone too far. For instance, as mentioned earlier, NAMA host countries are not necessarily interested in privatizing their strategic infrastructure. Should such privatization even come at a premium, in order to attract foreign instead of local investors, the leveraging exercise may become somewhat contentious.

In the (interim) absence of aggregators, the hybrid institutions could lend themselves to the objective due to their nature – public financing for private investment. In that respect both the equity investors –development finance institutions like IFC and a number of similar institutions – and the ECAs could stand in for an aggregator role until such function is established in the market. Alternatively, and most likely better, they could become integrated parts of an aggregation system for NAMAs.

The guarantee system and its shortcomings

As mentioned in Chapter 5, the Climate Policy Initiative (CPI) launched a series of risk gap analyses in January 2013 stating that 'currently, gaps in risk coverage hinder renewable energy investments. Risk — whether real or perceived — is in fact the single most important factor preventing renewable energy projects from finding financial investors, or raising the returns that these investors demand.' According to the CPI, in developing markets, as with developed markets, there is a gap in policy risk coverage. Financing risks are higher than in developed markets, due to immature financial institutions and markets, and are insufficiently covered by existing instruments. 'Concessional resources address these financial risks at the project level, but so far have not addressed liquidity risks. Two types of instruments can address some of these risk coverage gaps — first-loss protection instruments and policy risk insurance' (CPI). Not all risks need to be covered by insurance. If a risk can be avoided altogether there is no need to pay for its coverage. Risks that cannot be avoided need covering through guarantee products. If there are no guarantee products in the market to address a given risk, the last resort is to manage the risk. That typically means limiting the potential damage to a manageable minimum. Ultimately, if this minimum damage is too severe, the project will not materialize. A policy NAMA could possibly bring former unmanageable risks into a category, where they can be mitigated. Even though this is unlikely to be the typical formulation of a NAMA objective it might well be a very efficient one.

The central institutions for the provision of such guarantee products are the ECAs, which offer classical export credit – the reasoning behind the creation of the institutions, in the first place – and the investment-related guarantees addressed by the CPI. More advanced ECAs operating as government-owned 'exim' banks, can also offer direct lending with a relatively longer financing horizon (but not much more appetite for risk than normal banks).

The classical guarantees transform assets into liquidity through the intervention of commercial banks or other financial actors. Pension funds, for instance, or public (development) banks may also lend against a guarantee issued by an ECA. The range of possible identities of the counterpart depends on the specific guarantee. There are guarantees without recourse to an exporter, a 'supplier's credit insurance' where an exporting vendor of a product offers his buyer a credit. He refinances this credit in his own bank through a credit insurance with an ECA. The opposite structure is a 'buyer's credit insurance' where the buyer draws a loan from his own bank to pay for the equipment. The ECA of the country where the equipment is bought offers a credit insurance to the local bank. These types of guarantees are also used in project financing structures and functions as a counterparty risk – the fourth step in Figure 10.

A third product is 'working capital guarantees', which could be relevant for the financial engineering of a NAMA promoting a larger scale roll-out of a given technology, say solar PV lamps in the hundreds of thousands. There are other products like exporter's bonds (covering the exporters warrants towards the buyer in case of prepayment) and performance or warranty bonds (covering technology risk) that cover the buyer's unwarranted call of such bonds.

These classical risk products from the export credit agencies are useful, but insufficient. The most important shortcoming is that they are largely unavailable to the typical investor in activities that are promoted by a NAMA: the domestic investor in the NAMA host country – not an exporter from a developed country, or a foreign investor. The 'raison d'être' for these institutions is the cross-border trade or investment – essentially a developed country export promotion system that is not designed for NAMA host country domestic investors. Even the guarantees offered by the Multilateral Investment Guarantee Agency (MIGA), which is a part of the World Bank group, target cross-border transactions. A product like MIGA's expropriation coverage, for instance, is available only to the foreign investor even though a domestic investor faces an identical risk.[2]

The role of local companies, finance, and equipment in climate projects, even in developing countries, is being underestimated – and the CDM is the case in point. The ECA's current ceiling for local cost or content of up to 30 per cent simply does not match the typical project and ownership structure. This is not a question of 30 or 50 per cent, it is a matter of offering guarantee products for the larger majority of projects that are in the hands of NAMA host countries' local developers. It is not the guarantees for those developed country equipment suppliers who take out insurance against buyers' non-payment, but the guarantees that cover the nationalization or other less severe regulatory risks pertaining to the entire investment, that are in demand. Could such limitations on ECA guarantees be relaxed? If so, under which conditions? Which tranches of risk cover should be considered? A reduction of the share of national content would expand the reach of the ECAs – but a full elimination could be the ultimate solution to many other issues, and respond to the idea that the most efficient way to apply financing for NAMAs is as far back in the financing value chain as possible.

Not knowing the origin of the equipment at the time of guarantee issuance, has previously prompted unsuccessful ideas of 'clearing houses' or common guarantee structures among the ECAs. Temporary climate guarantees offered by a central institution – for instance, established by a group of countries agreeing to place a given amount in a fund structure, such as the Green Climate Fund – could effectively constitute a re-launch of an old non-starter. But could the climate agenda finally bring it to life? If it is based on firm agreements to transfer issued risk cover from the interim climate guarantee issuer to the relevant ECA, once project and equipment has been identified, it would allow the ECAs a central role in securing significant amounts of climate funding. It should be noted that the ECAs can enter into co-insurance and re-insurance arrangements with one another, as well as with other financing and guarantee sources. This is not compromising the national export promotion focus, but rather a quite cumbersome replacement for an ideal 'global ECA', which would offer guarantees like those outlined above, but without any national bindings.

All this is circumventions, however, and does not solve the central challenge, which is that NAMA host countries' project developers, for their own domestic investment purposes, do not have any decent equivalent to the ECAs. These investments, as documented by the CDM, are more than 90 per cent of the investment activity. Hence, in reality, the gap in risk cover identified by the CPI is much larger.

In previous chapters, it was argued that the transformational changes sought through the establishment of NAMAs were linked to permanent changes in the way cash flows give priority to certain types of activities. The cash flows are, by and large, a result of the preferences established by government regulation. For many NAMAs that promote investment in higher cost investment alternatives, the NAMA host government may (have to) support the higher cost alternative through a subsidy.

According to the principles for financial engineering established in the previous chapter, a relatively efficient way of injecting such subsidies would be through a partial support of a cash flow. ECAs are familiar with securitization of the regulation-based cash flows, but only in a narrow band of common products – in this respect notably the sales of electricity. Even a very common cash flow relevant to climate projects, namely the feed-in tariff, is not sufficiently common for ECAs to offer guarantees for a feed-in tariff-based cash flow. The exception to the rule is American Overseas Private Investment Corporation's (OPIC) feed-in tariff insurance, which has successfully secured remedies from host governments, obtaining compensation when breaches have occurred. However, the public sector toolbox for the promotion of renewable energy or other climate friendly technologies is much larger, and comprises depreciation rules, tax holidays, removal of subsidies, etc. All of these play a role in establishing profitability of the lower emission alternative – which would greatly increase their value if they could be secured. In the current market, they cannot.

If NAMA host country national budgets are the starting point for designing the financial base, normally in the form of cash flows, for both public and private investments in climate change mitigation, why do ECAs not yet have any dedicated products to safeguard these cash flows? Some of the relevant, and missing, instruments are directly linked to projects, while others are linked to general framework conditions. Removing subsidies to competing technologies, or technology standards that force investment into efficient technologies are policies that influence long-term development in a sector, and not necessarily the single investment. Could a general business environment even be insured, assuming that foreign investors, in particular, would establish themselves on the basis of a portfolio development plan? In which way can ECAs insure any of these instruments, so as to make them more reliable for the private sector investor – and, thus, a basis for NAMA implementation?

Many climate investments in NAMA host countries are relatively small-scale and would not attract the interest of banks, due to higher relative transaction costs. Figure 8 includes credit lines, which may originate from a development bank, but will, in any case, be administered by a local bank in a NAMA host country. It is a common structure that would be relevant for smaller scale private sector climate investments, motivated by government regulation. Could ECAs make guarantee products available for small-scale climate actions? Could the bundling of projects or a higher degree of standardization be considered? Could government shopping lines be an option (i.e., the NAMA host government buys on behalf of the end users and possibly establishes a national lending programme)?

Stronger market actors take on the accumulation themselves, like energy service companies (ESCOs) that build up portfolios of smaller energy efficiency investments, and profit from savings on energy (and emissions). These are often highly efficient climate investments, particularly in energy efficiency, but they are not straightforward cases for the ECAs, even though ECAs have been known to offer shopping lines to large clients for the purchase of predefined equipment. Applying such criteria is an alternative to project-by-project evaluation.

Standardized due diligence is another option. It is imaginable that governments, when imposing new regulations that require market actors to invest – e.g., compulsory exchange of inefficient pumps – would offer a financing arrangement, thus, in practice, offering a shopping line for the private sector to draw on. Could such a structure be guaranteed? Who would be liable for repayment? What sort of risk cover could ECAs provide in this set-up? Is it required?

Energy efficiency investments are recognized as the most efficient, and profitable, emissions reduction options. However, because they are marginal to the core business, they simply do not happen. ESCOs, as mentioned above, have energy efficiency as their core business, but there are particular risks involved that need to be covered. In the building sector, which is one of the areas where ESCOs do operate, there are additional issues of securitizing revenues, collateral (equipment is built into the building) and legal aspects of interrupting supply. To overcome barriers to ESCO involvement, ESCOs could be legally required partners of developers of new buildings. In such a model, the developer can leave the project as normal, but the ESCO would be the investor in the climate shield or 'building envelope' and heating/cooling equipment, and be secured with a 5 to 10 year contract to operate the building, based on a traditional ESCO model. Could ECAs cover the ESCOs regulatory, (supplier) performance or other risks, in such structures? If ECAs streamline and reduce the cost of risk cover, it could affect the private sector's investment appetite for smaller scale projects.

The bottom line for all of these options is that they are still only possibilities, not readily available off-the-shelf insurance products, which they need to be before they can make a real difference in NAMA finance. Their claim to the NAMA finance label would lie in their breakaway from business as usual, and the mandates that govern the ECAs.

The ECAs as aggregators

The true perspectives for the financial engineering of NAMAs lie in strategic leveraging of instruments and financiers. 'Blending' was described in the previous chapter for an avenue involving a number of different financiers in different roles, perhaps guided by an 'aggregator' that, beyond fund raising, would also assume the role of adviser. In the absence of institutions filling the aggregators' role the hybrid finance institutions and possibly the ECAs may be candidates for the provision of advice on the financial engineering of a NAMA. Do ECAs possess the competencies – and could they assume the role without risking conflicts of interest? What steps should be taken in order to place ECAs in that central position?

The ECAs would be familiar with most financiers' due diligence processes – they have their own as well. Also, the ECAs will benefit from their position being the furthest back in the financing value chain. Their financial involvement, including possible climate change related instruments provided by their developed country host governments, would cascade down through the financing value chain, leveraging other sources of finance. Like most other financial institutions they are familiar with risk assessment, but obviously more so than other financiers, as they are in the business of valuating and pricing it. They are, therefore, well positioned as advisers to NAMA host governments with respect to eliminating sources of risk in their regulatory frameworks – regulatory elements that often may be removed at no cost. They are also in a foremost position as advisers, due to the obvious effect of not following their advice: Investments cannot be insured or the guarantee premiums will (remain) prohibitive. NAMA host governments could mistake this for 'hostage taking', but in reality it would probably be the most valuable piece of advice they could get.

The most important difference is that the focus of most financing activity in the ECAs and other hybrid institutions is on project financing. NAMAs, instead, will commonly require models for policy financing – models for the provision of the permanent cash flows that are to underpin the transformational changes. It is exactly the securitization of such cash flows that make the ECAs possibly the most obvious candidate for assuming the role of aggregators. While other financiers, mostly those with a focus on private sector investment, will engage in project financing (which in this context is not regarded as NAMA finance) the ECAs would help establish the investment framework, through the provision of (policy) guarantee models (which then *would* be regarded as NAMA finance).

A disadvantage, by contrast, could be that the ECAs are generally unfamiliar with the climate change agenda and the affiliated institutions – and vice versa. There is a gap between the institutions and programmes that register themselves in the UNFCCC NAMA Registry as financiers of NAMAs, and the private financial sector that the ECAs are more closely linked to. The Registry platform is established with the official purpose of matching NAMAs with funding. However, it is not, and will not likely be, known in broader financing sector circles, thus unfortunately underpinning an assumption that NAMA financing is treated as donor funding and specifically of the grant variation. Moreover, it underscores the differentiation and not the integration of financing. The ECAs would need to penetrate the international climate financing discussions and its approaches to NAMA finance to assume an efficient aggregator role.

Mandates

Many financing institutions relevant for NAMA support are old institutions with old mandates. None of these are created for the financing of climate related projects, let alone NAMAs. They operate on the basis of mandates that are designed for other purposes. A typical mandate is that of the World

Bank and the International Development Agency (IDA), which is the World Bank's concessional lending instrument. Established in 1960, the IDA offers concessional lending to the world's 82 poorest countries on the basis of criteria that relate to indices, first and foremost a GNI per capita below an annually updated threshold (in the fiscal year 2014: $1,205). The IDA charges little or no interest and repayments are stretched over 25 to 40 years, including a 5- to 10-year grace period. It is the single largest source of donor funds for basic social services in these countries. For the fiscal year ending on June 30, 2013, the IDA commitments reached USD 16.3 billion 15 per cent of which was committed on grant terms.

The IDA also supports some countries, including several small island economies, that are above the operational cutoff but lack the creditworthiness needed to borrow from the World Bank's normal lending windows. Some countries, such as India and Pakistan, are IDA-eligible based on per capita income levels, and are also creditworthy for some borrowing from the World Bank. They are referred to as 'blend' countries.

Thus, eligibility criteria are already bended. Given that climate change affects all regardless of the location of the emissions source, would it be unimaginable to revise the IDA's mandate to being purpose-specific and not simply country specific, within certain limits? Many NAMAs would undoubtedly benefit immensely from concessional lending – corresponding to support of the finance in Figure 14. The IDA has no option, however, to deviate from the mandate. Under the catchy heading 'managing the unavoidable, avoiding the unmanageable' IDA is 'helping the poorest nations adapt by building their resilience to disasters'. With a revised mandate, it could add NAMAs as part of the strategy for 'avoiding the unmanageable', regardless of GNI figures.

To avoid competition among treasuries of their host governments, ECAs are tightly regulated institutions. The 'Arrangement on Guidelines for Officially Supported Export Credits' seeks to harmonize the support that the ECAs offer for goods or services contracts with a repayment term of 2 years or more, which they base on 'consensus rules' that make changes a very tedious process. Clearly, this tight regulation is detrimental to unconstrained business development – it is supposed to be – but in this case, it is also detrimental to the development of guarantee products in support of the climate cause. With a few tweaks, if permitted, the reach of the ECAs would be significantly increased, as indicated by the series of questions raised above.

The investment guarantees offered by the ECAs are not covered by the consensus rules which, conversely, means that in investment guarantees, commercial risks – which *are* covered by the consensus rules – generally cannot be covered. The important exception to this rule is a breach of contract by a government-dominated institution – i.e., not necessarily a fully government owned one. Such contracts may be concessions or Power Purchase Agreements (PPAs) with a corporatized national utility. These guarantee products, which are steps two and three in Figure 10, are particularly useful for the financial engineering of NAMAs that concern the private investment in, and operation of, renewable energy installations, for example.

Generally, ECAs providing credit guarantees can manage longer credit terms than commercial lenders. Different sectors have different limitations; credit guarantees for particularly durable assets have a guarantee limitation of 18 years, maximum. In supporting Danish investors and technology export interests, the Danish ECA, EKF, successfully advocated the extending of the general 12-year limit, to up to 18 years maximum to cover wind energy assets. However, the system is rigid. The exception for wind turbines took years to negotiate, and when finally agreed also covered solar PV, biomass and other equally relevant and durable technologies. Preferential treatment is being extended to other areas under a climate heading, serving as an example of 'mandate tweaking', and other flexible repayment profiles could have merit in the support of private climate investments promoted by a NAMA.[3]

ECAs are mandated to cover only (up to) 80 per cent of senior debt, thus, leaving 20 per cent, or more, to higher priced risk cover, alternatively not covered. Partial cover is one of the ways in which the ECAs are able to control the price of risk cover. The ECAs' primary distribution channels are the commercial banks, which typically accept a small self-insurance of about 5 to 10 per cent of the loan, when the buyer's credit guarantee is practically unconditional. But the hybrid finance institutions accept other, more risky models. ECAs also insure the hybrid financiers, and other financiers such as pension funds, supra-national banks, like the European Investment bank or development banks, or climate funds. If a project is located in a country in risk category six or seven, for instance, the ECA may suggest that a project loan be split in two. The ECA would then cover the 50 per cent unconditional, while the remaining 50 per cent would not be covered – or 'self-insured' by the hybrid. In that way, the pricing of the 50 per cent risk remains manageable in the project finance structure. Such splits could incorporate sovereign guarantee elements from the NAMA host government for the portion that is not covered by the ECA – although the reason for the split, in the first place, is that the investment climate, including the host government's regulatory framework, is regarded as too unfriendly and, thus, too expensive to insure. As such, a sovereign guarantee may not have much value.

Expanding the reach of the ECAs products through a widening of its mandate will obviously come at a cost. Lowering the premiums, extending maturities, increasing cover percentages all has a cost that, if not borne by the market must be borne by the ECAs' backing governments. A recent push in that direction is missing the point, however. Recent imposition of grant elements for public sector buyers has caused a number of government deals to shipwreck due to lack of funding options from ECA host governments. Effectively, this means that the ECAs have to provide grants out of their operational budgets – unless they can convince their owners, which are their host governments' national treasuries, to reimburse the grant. While the objective may be noble, the grant requirement has de facto prompted what the ECA regulations are meant to prevent: a competition between ECA host government treasuries. On the other hand, if consensus could be established on rules not only for the provision of such grants, but also for their reimbursement, the model is de facto a support for the guarantee system which in the previous chapter was identified as the most efficient way to inject climate finance into NAMAs.

Most donor governments offer mixed credits (sometimes called soft loans), which are a subtype of concessional loans that are regulated by the OECD Development Assistance Committee (DAC). Mixed credits are defined by the OECD as 'a credit that contains an aid element, so as to provide concessional credit terms – such as a lower rate of interest or a longer credit period'.[1] The transaction requires that the Ministry of Finance, or central bank of the importer's country, guarantees the loan or that another acceptable form of security is furnished. A few countries still tie these mixed credits to minimum supplies stemming from the credit's country of origin, but the OECD has rooted out this practice in most countries.

A number of consensus standards – in this case, set by the DAC – are to create a level playing field and to prevent cases where countries offering these favourable terms do not venture into competition between national ministries of finance. However, as with the ECAs, the DAC 'one-size-fits-all' rules are not efficient from a NAMA financing and leveraging perspective. The DAC rules define a grant element of 35 per cent to be incorporated by the lender in the mixed credit loan agreement. For many years, interest levels have been so low that mixed credits, due to this regulation, have effectively provided interest-free loans, free ECA guarantees and, additionally, a grant supporting the asset. Such a fixed percentage disregards that projects and activities will require different levels of support to become bankable. Some – and probably most – projects require less than the 35 per cent grant element to become bankable, sometimes even significantly less. A 'mixed climate credit' *not* regulated by the OECD DAC consensus could be a valuable instrument for the financial engineering of NAMAs, with three main flexible parameters:

1) The grant percentage (e.g., 5 to 30 per cent)
2) The tenor (e.g., maximum 20 years)
3) The payment of the guarantee premium

The last parameter relates to the role that ECAs have in the mixed credit structure, which always involves a financing institution for the provision of the loan to which the grant element is added. Revising the mixed credit instrument will, therefore, also require a revision of the consensus rules governing the ECAs, with the purpose of ensuring that the ECAs may provide risk cover for a mixed climate credit in the same manner, and on the same conditions, as the current mixed credits.

One of the most problematic mandates is the way in which general development assistance is administered. Developing countries are encouraged, through NAMAs, to initiate 'transformational' changes over the long term in their greenhouse gas emitting economic sectors. These require long-term financing plans, which developed countries are supposed to take part in. Developed countries' funding models, however, are only short-term annual allocations, and implementation periods rarely exceed five years – most often, less. This funding modus reduces its value significantly. It perpetuates exactly the impermanence that the NAMA host countries are encouraged to avoid through transformation. It is quite unthinkable that developed countries can change their principles for allocation of assistance from an annual finance bill provision – guided by the 0.7 per cent of GDP target, but often challenged by financial constraints and domestic priorities – to a steady flow of funds based on, e.g., 20-year commitments. However, if instead a share of the allocation is channelled into the ECAs as guarantee capital for a dedicated climate guarantee fund, the annual allocations accumulate in a permanent structure that can secure long-term finance and possibly long-term cash flows. Allocations could be a fixed percentage of annual climate finance budgets allowing the ECAs to constantly increase their climate guarantee activities. Assuming guarantees are not called, at a rate higher than normal, the fund could either be revolving or it could incorporate the grant elements that have recently been imposed so unsuccessfully.

This modus would specifically address, although not entirely cover, the financing gap identified in Chapter 7. It would allow the establishment of a grant-based guarantee structure for cash flows, but it would not constitute the cash flow itself – unless someone would experiment with negative guarantee premiums. Such cash flows probably have to originate in the NAMA host countries' national budgets, which, so far, remain the only platform that can ensure their relative permanence.

There are ways in which such national budgets can be bolstered, however. One of the most promising developments in that respect is the emergence of the green bonds. This is an efficient financing instrument that allows the institutional investors a role, possibly even a significant role over time, in the provision of patient finance for climate investment and, thus, also for NAMAs. In the following chapter, the Green Climate Fund is used as a generic label for actions and instruments that the Fund, with significant advantages, could engage in. However, it does not have to be the GCF. The functions and instruments could also be hosted and administered by other institutions – a virtual alternative to a centralized and all-encompassing GCF, which is at risk of duplicating instruments that are already in the market, instead of ensuring that these existing institutions may increase their reach and effect through a change or revision of their mandates.

Summing Up

Given that guarantees, from a leveraging point of view, are the most efficient intervention to activate as much mainstream financing for NAMAs as possible, this chapter has decidedly focused on guarantees and the particular shortcomings in the market for guarantee products. One of the most important shortfalls is the limited access to risk cover for local investors in NAMA host countries. As the typical private investor in a NAMA host country – also for actions promoted by a NAMA – is local, this shortfall must be addressed. While the ECAs are not necessarily the ones to do so, adjustments to their mandates could multiply their relevance for local investors.

Mandates are generally what hinder many financing institutions, relevant for provision of NAMA finance, from delivering their part. Most tools have already been invented; they only need to be applied in new contexts, or with more flexible mandates motivated by the climate agenda.

Chapter 9

ROLES OF THE GREEN
CLIMATE FUND

The Green Climate Fund (GCF) is still a work in progress, but it has the potential to become a decisive player in global climate finance. It is thought to eventually become a financial supermarket – which may or may not be desirable – offering loans, equity and guarantees in accordance with market demands. As a new organization, it does not have any accumulated experience in providing such instruments as yet; however, such experience can be acquired. It would be unfortunate if the GCF ultimately draws up a shopping list that essentially duplicates existing offers in the market. Recalling the 'non-quote' in Chapter 4, there *is* likely sufficient financing available to undertake the necessary investments; however, the framework conditions that determine its deployment need to be improved. This may sound overly simplistic, but the current donor financiers have not yet found the key to unlocking the traditional financial markets – or the key is not compatible with the way they traditionally deploy their assistance.

The GCF Governing Instrument states that, 'financing will be provided to cover the identifiable additional costs of the investment necessary to make the project viable.' Intuitively this is sensible, but it is far from operational. A clearer guidance is required on how to assess 'additional costs', and who is affected by them, along with references to the former definition of NAMA finance. It seems to refer to the investment cost, in which case the GCF is indicating an intention to invest in physical assets – presumably on conditions similar to the GEF, i.e., without taking up any ownership. If this will ultimately be its mode of intervention, not only will it have chosen the most expensive and least efficient intervention model, it will also have duplicated the GEF. That is not what the market needs. Furthermore, it does not qualify what viable means, either. There are many viable projects that are not bankable, due to risk perceptions and lack of sufficient risk guarantee.

The financial products offered by the GCF to cover these additional costs have yet to be determined and the GCF, therefore, has all the options to inject itself with tailored assistance that is complementary to what is already available on the market. Financial instruments are to be approved by the GCF Board and may evolve over time and vary over financing windows. Grants and concessional loans are traditional and 'safe' products readily available on the market and therefore not complementary and of less consequence for leveraging climate finance – depending on how it is applied.

As already established and elaborated at length, the most efficient deployment model includes guarantees and instruments that can ensure the long-term financing of cash flows channelled through NAMA host countries' national operational budgets. A prime focus for a guarantee product from the GCF would target the domestic markets in NAMA host countries. This may or may not be done in collaboration with the existing ECAs, but there are obvious opportunities for collaboration, even with little adjustment of the consensus rules for the ECAs.

Before discussing the possible modes of intervention by the GCF, it is useful to present an investment structure to illustrate the different roles of different stakeholders. Figure 16 illustrates an example of a cash flow system that includes some of the instruments that have been discussed throughout the chapters, in an expanded securitization model. It illustrates a private supplier of public goods on a contract with a government – not because this is the only option, but because it is one that most clearly demonstrates options for optimizing funds deployment. The model is expanded with the possible roles of finance partners, including the GCF, illustrating options for cash flows surrounding the asset. It is, therefore, an example of what could be the result of a NAMA – although it could just as well illustrate current cash flows in a system, where a private entity – the Special Purpose Vehicle (SPV) in Figure 16 – is operating an asset with an undesirable emission profile, e.g., an inefficient coal fired power plant. The structure is equally useful in illustrating a pre-investment undesirable situation, as it is in illustrating the desirable change in preferences, through alterations of the cash flows.

This securitization model is familiar to those who embarked on private infrastructure in the 1990s with significant inspiration from the World Bank and incredible growth in the BOT market (Build Own/Operate, Transfer) in South East Asia and to some extent also in Latin America. While the BOT fell out of fashion and into infamy due to one too many tales of developing countries being taken advantage of by private developers, the Public Private Partnerships (PPPs) have risen to become the new model for collaboration between the public and private sectors. The founding principles are identical, however, the principle of 'partnership' only emphasizes what prudent developers were already adopting in the 1990s. The PPP emphasises a more active role for the public sector, notwithstanding the political processes that have surmounted the political barriers to involving the private sector in delivery of public goods.

Figure 16. Expanded securitization model

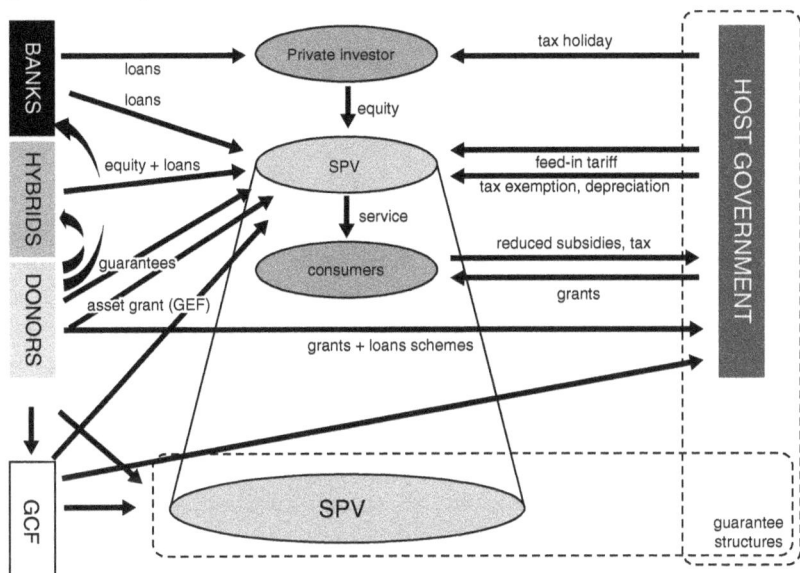

Private infrastructure is equal to other businesses, in the sense that it produces a service that is sold to consumers. However, the infrastructure supplier is often in a priority position, either as the sole supplier of certain goods, or being the supplier of goods that are in demand – or both. This puts them in a vulnerable position as well. Transport, water and energy supply, which affect the general public, are politically sensitive and, thus, they are often the object of national grants in the form of subsidies. Privatization commonly includes plans for tariff increases to a level that ensures profitability. Despite the best-stated intentions, this may prove politically unacceptable. Fossil fuel subsidies, for instance, are a very hard habit to break. For that reason, it cannot be assumed that any desirable project can eventually be made profitable and bankable through the engineering of a least cost equity, loan and guarantee package that optimizes risk/return ratios. As stated in Chapter 1, the financial engineering of a NAMA cannot make the incremental cost disappear.

The securitization model in Figure 16 includes some, but not all, of the instruments that have been listed as part of the NAMA host country's regulatory toolbox and not all of those instruments that may be, or may be made, available through the institutions that claim to be willing to participate in climate or NAMA financing. Reiterating the climate finance and particularly the NAMA finance definition, there really is no particular NAMA finance in a profitable investment with a desirable emission profile; the NAMA finance is in the instrument that makes such investments profitable. The GCF may be one of the central vehicles for the delivery of such 'instrument financing', but it would be doing so in partnership with other institutions with expertise in the relevant niches.

The Green Climate Fund and Risk

To the extent that the GCF intends to provide guarantees – and it should, given the efficiency of such interventions – a fast-track option could be the involvement of the ECAs. They would, effectively, operate the GCF guarantee window, based on their own funds – or additional funds allocated by national governments to the ECAs for the dedicated operation of the GCF window. It could be operationalized through a reinforcement of ECA resources, while capitalizing on existing routines and expertise. Such a linkage might also be an encouragement for the ECAs to offer climate guarantees, themselves. Alternatively, exploiting the ECAs' current market position, the GCF could consider offering reinsurance where ECAs could seek partial coverage of their exposure through a guarantee instrument provided by the GCF – although a general reinsurance of the ECA guarantees would not help, as it would neither change the ECAs' risk assessment, nor the actual (or perceived) project risk, nor improve on the sovereign character of the ECA risk cover. However, a broader risk distribution effort, possibly including other institutions like the multilateral and bilateral development banks, could explore 'economies of scale', as well as generally expanding the guarantee offer in the market through such partnerships.

The GCF could also offer an expansion of the existing coverage of the ECA guarantees. The GCF could cover the parts of a given project that go beyond the ECAs' limitations. An extension of the local costs content could be an attractive option for NAMAs based on locally manufactured technologies; coverage over and above the standard 80 per cent senior debt coverage would also be a straightforward case that could improve bank lending through a reduction in their risk exposure.

The increased local cost coverage, ideally in full, may involve the direct collaboration with the NAMA host country, for instance in co-insurance or reinsurance together with the NAMA host government, maximizing the host country's leveraging of a number of other investors and lenders. Expanding the coverage beyond 80 per cent would also be attractive, due to its ease of implementation, as the risk assessment has already been undertaken by the ECA.

Some marginal cases that the ECAs are reluctant to absorb, like documentation risks or lenders' negligence, often would not be covered in securitization structures. They could, however, be objects for reinsurance by the GCF, hence, enhancing the ECAs' ability to offer guarantees for such securitization structures (see Figure 16). The GCF could decide to take on such risks without much risk assessment, relying only on an ECA recommendation. Other types of risks that the ECAs do not cover, which are clear objects for GCF involvement, are changes in framework conditions that do *not* stem from changes of law – for instance, subtle changes in practices of law enforcement, which (normally) would be beyond coverage from the ECAs. This would be an area where the GCF would be particularly well suited as guarantor, due to the direct linkage to the climate agenda. Non-enforcement of a NAMA structure has repercussions not only for potential investors, but also for the host country's standing in the donor community, for attraction of other NAMA-related financing – and possibly the standing in international climate negotiations. Here, the GCF would be a central player, whereas the ECAs would be marginal to non-existent in this context.

A precondition for these collaborative risk cover options between the ECAs and the GCF, is that the GCF would have a rating based either on its founding rules or on its standing, particularly the safety cushions established by national Treasuries for the GCFs uncovered payment obligations, if any. This would entail a simple counterparty risk assessment, as the ECA would need to assess the dependability of the reinsurance.

The guarantee options listed here, as well as in the ECA section, are all targeting risk cover for the private sector in its engagement with the public sector. However, not only is there risk aversion in the private sector; the public sector – likely with some justification – is equally risk averse when contracting with the private sector for long-term infrastructure services. The private sector involvement, during the 1990s, in the infrastructure market left many developing country governments with negative experiences. Consequently, many public sector executives in developing countries might find that while the private sector is preoccupied with risk avoidance and risk mitigation, nobody seems to be concerned with the public sector's risk in contracting with the private sector. In depth examination looks at the faux pas of the public sector's sudden retroactive change of contract conditions, not the private contractor's claim that certain conditions have changed and charges consequently must go up. Undoubtedly, the private sector's access to legal advice, and willingness to use it, by far exceeds that of the public sector, and many developing countries have had to realize this the hard way. There is simply a gap in risk cover for the public sector.

As previously mentioned, another shortcoming is the ECA system's applicability only to the foreign direct investment. For domestic investors in NAMA host countries, investment guarantees are notoriously difficult to obtain, often with the requirement that an amount in cash, similar to the size of the guarantee, is deposited in a bank. Such a guarantee is obviously worthless.

However, national investors are equally exposed to risks of changes in national regulations, for instance, compared to their foreign counterparts. Supporting national guarantee structures could release local private sector investments, and at the same time put national investors on an equal footing with foreign investors in joint projects. Moreover, it could reduce the local cost of capital, where equity positions are often rewarded with annual returns of 25 per cent or more – which is not alarming when comparing to the cost of capital, following Figure 10. Such levels are natural reflections of the investment risks, whether perceived or real.

There are several options for the GCF to provide risk cover that is not currently available in the market. It should be done, however, not as a new separate provider of guarantees with a full-fledged guarantee programme. Instead, it should be done in close collaboration with already existing government-backed ECAs, to find the niche(s) within which its enhancement of existing guarantee products would bring about new NAMA finance.

The Green Climate Fund and Green Bonds

The greatest possible challenge to NAMA financing – and the one that the donor community is unable to fill through its current practice – is the provision of long-term cash flows. Transformational changes of a sector require a transformation of the cash flows – quite often increased cash flows. The public sector's challenge is to finance such cash flows through the public coffers. Engaging the private sector through a securitization model like the one illustrated in Figure 16, relieves the public sector from raising investment capital, though it is left with the obligation of securing cash flows that make the private sector investment profitable. The profitability depends on the price of capital – and capital in NAMA host countries can be expensive. The public sector may, therefore, consider whether it can play an active role in reducing the cost of capital. One of the instruments could be green bonds.

A bond differs from other loans in the sense that it is not governed by a loan agreement. Instead, it is issued for the primary market at an exchange. The issuer receives cash proceeds from the sale. After issuance, the bond is traded between investors in the secondary market exchange, giving price indications for a fixed coupon through a pricing of the bond. The price reflects the risk and the demand, and liquidity of the bond.

Green bonds have been in the market for some time. But who are they for? According to the Climate Bonds Initiative (CBI), only 3 per cent of climate bonds currently in the market are project bonds, while 82 per cent are corporate bonds, and 2 per cent are municipal bonds. The remaining 13 per cent are financial bonds from institutions such as the World Bank. Although they only represent 3 per cent of the current market, green bonds are a relevant choice for long-term financing of large-scale renewable energy projects – hydro, wind, solar. In developing countries, however, most climate investments are not large scale, and few would justify taking the bond route, since bonds rely on tradability and market liquidity. In most NAMA host countries, a project-by-project approach would not be feasible. The municipality-backed bond issuance is also only a fraction of the green bond market, and is likely not the route for NAMA host governments either. However, if national governments take on a role in bond issuance, raising capital through the bonds market, and on-lending it for national climate actions implemented by the private sector, it could, theoretically, reduce the cost of capital for the private service provider and, thus, also the cost of the service provided. An example of both a national and regional green bond in potential NAMA host countries is given in the text box, presenting the Southern African Power Pool. The example applies the financing value chain approach, asking that *if* the product is a green bond, what would be the instruments and actors necessary to activate it in that context?

In a simple model, the financing of a number of renewable energy installations in the Southern African Power Pool could consist of 30 per cent equity and 70 per cent climate bonds. This structure is used for the loan financing of a portfolio of mutually supportive wind and hydro investments in the SAPP – see Figure 17.

The cost of finance is also influenced by the equity requirement. In less risky investment climates, like in Northern Europe, it goes as low as 20 per cent even for renewable energy. In less mature markets it may go as high as 50 per cent. The equity requirement is set by the lenders as a cushion against risk. In this case, the issuer of the bond, SAPP (through, e.g., Southern African Development Bank or South Africa's Industrial Development Corporation) backed by its member governments, guarantees to repay the bond over a certain period of time. SAPP, being a government backed institution on-lending the bond revenues to the pool of renewable energy projects, may decide to lower the demand for equity (in this case to 30 per cent but it could also be lower) as it may assess the risk of its own default on the power purchase agreements with the renewable energy suppliers as negligible.

The structure clearly has to be acceptable to the buyer of the bond. So far, green bonds are priced higher than ordinary corporate bonds due to lower acceptability in the market and higher perceived risks. If the risk premium becomes too high, the ECAs could be instrumental in bringing them down. However, large bond issuances that are not project specific, but only based on general investment criteria, cannot currently be enhanced or risk covered through an ECA. Such issuances typically succeed through large development banks, like the World Bank, although here it is proposed as a regional initiative.

Currently, there are few, if any, institutions that would routinely assume the role of bond issuer on the basis of an aggregation of similar activities – i.e., bonds that finance either a specific portfolio of projects, or an open-ended floating of bonds in tranches or series. Such models exist for housing markets in a number of countries, where a very large pool of relatively small housing investments are aggregated and financed through the issuance of bonds in series. The aggregation spreads the risk over thousands of assets, not only for the bonds investor, but also for the aggregator that issues the bonds.

This constitutes an obvious market opening for the GCF. The GCF might issue bonds in its own name in large non-project-specific tranches for loan financing of NAMAs, although it will, to some extent, be a duplication of a role that the World Bank and other development banks are already fulfilling. The difference might be in the branding of green bonds from the Green Climate Fund, but it may also choose to enhance the bonds with additional risk cover for project portfolios that the ECAs are unable to cover. It could attempt a self-insurance strategy, although it would, in the same way as the ECAs, be met with a 100 per cent guarantee demand for the entire bond issuance, which it would not be able to honour unless it had unlimited drawing rights on the contributors' (donors) finance ministries, effectively lending a sovereign status to the bond. However, this may be exactly the kind of NAMA finance that would most efficiently reduce the cost of climate friendly infrastructure services in NAMA host countries.

If this should prove too risky for the donor countries' finance ministries, who are more comfortable with predictable annual budgets for development and climate assistance, the ECAs can perhaps guarantee such bonds – if they are 'quasi-sovereign';[1] they may guarantee part of the bond (having a guaranteed and a non-guaranteed bond issuance[2]). Otherwise, they may insure the on-lending case by case for specific investments, if they find the foundation of a particular project sufficiently strong. Alternatively, if the ECAs should offer full guarantees, the result would normally be that any price advantage created via the enhanced rating of the bond would partly, or even in total, be consumed by the premium paid for ECA guarantee.

The GCF might decide on a project specifically to be self-insured, to save the cost of the involvement of the ECAs. But unless the GCF is willing to put large shareholdings on the line (which would counter its leveraging objective) it cannot venture into activities that are much riskier than the market would otherwise consider, simply because in doing so it would have great difficulty finding any co-investors. The involvement of ECAs would be in jeopardy, should the GCF decide against self-insurance or depend on other co-investors

Green bonds in the Southern African Power Pool

The Southern African Power Pool (SAPP) is an excellent example of a region with ideal conditions for large-scale wind energy. The SAPP consists of nine grid connected countries (and three that are not connected). Three of these nine are almost exclusively fossil fuel-based, while the remaining six are predominantly hydropower-based. Transmission lines are sufficient for the current capacity exchanges, but would need reinforcement for significant capacity increases. South Africa and Namibia, which are fossil-fuel-based, have excellent wind resources; Mozambique, Zambia and Zimbabwe have significant hydropower resources, with plans for expansion that can also be used as storage capacity for large penetration rates of intermittent capacity, like wind energy. Large-scale wind energy investments are under preparation -- these might be pooled with even more mature hydropower technology investments for parallel investment programmes. For the financing of the expansion programmes, the SAPP countries could embark on a large, international renewable energy programme, based on a large-scale floating of green bonds backed by the SAPP governments and secured by, e.g., the GCF.

that would require ECA involvement, since ECAs do not assume risks beyond a given, but not generally determinable, limit. In other words, the ECAs can enhance a good risk, but they cannot turn a bad risk into a good one. And neither can the GCF.

Bringing the insurer on board for the climate bond may be a necessary interim alternative to standardization. While the insurer is used to project specific risk assessment, the market is used to standards. Climate bond standardization is being worked on in different contexts. The Climate Bonds Initiative has developed the Climate Bonds Standard, which is 'a tool that helps investors verify the climate effectiveness of their investments'. A standard would help rating agencies evaluating the bonds through generally accepted ratings, ultimately mainstreaming the climate bonds into the existing bonds market.

Bond issuance, instead of bank loans, could also be 'mixed' with the mixed credit, possibly through a general bond issuance by the mixed credit host country. In that case, it would be a developed country government green bond. Mixed credits with green bond financing could be an option for the GCF to activate the institutional investors in supported finance. The grant element addressing the fact that financing to cover an incremental cost, in

Figure 17. Simple investment structure involving green bonds

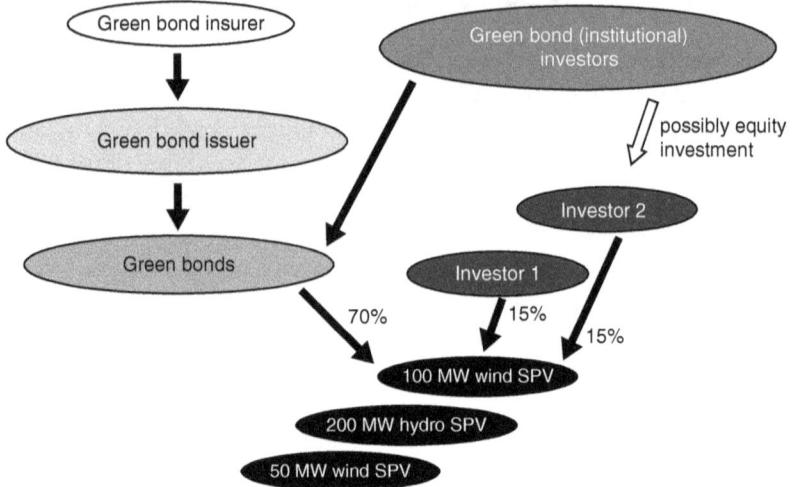

whichever way and wherever it materializes in the financing structure or securitization model, is not an investment. It is a constant drain, and the financing to cover it may have to be injected somewhere in the financing plan. The choice stands between the four distinct levels in the financing value chain. Due to its nature – a constant drain – it will have to be provided by national or international public sector institutions as support of the asset (GEF incremental costs), support of the finance, or support of the risk cover through government-backed guarantees. The grant element in the mixed credit corresponds to support of the finance.

The Green Climate Fund and Equity

Before the GCF or other bilateral NAMA financiers establish yet another hybrid finance institution it should be considered which types of investments that current equity investors, including the hybrids, cannot or do not promote. There are natural limitations for such hybrids. They can never replace the project sponsor or developer. It was established above that the GCF cannot adopt a very different risk profile than the rest of the market, unless it wants to provide all the financing itself – so the establishment of a 'particularly risk taking' hybrid is not viable. The GCF might decide to help addressing a shortfall of local project development capacity by providing professional training or mentoring of local sponsors with an objective to develop local companies, but this obviously does not correspond to equity participation.

To differentiate itself from the hundreds of equity investors that are already available for investment in NAMA host countries, the GCF could possibly emulate an EU attempt to provide 'equity grants', which were to bolster equity investors when negotiating bank loans. The mechanics is that the most expensive capital, the equity, is bolstered by an additional amount of equity, which does not require any return on the investment at all. Increasing equity, from, e.g., 20 to 35 per cent, has significant impact on banks' risk assessment and, thus, on the price of financing; the price of risk cover also goes down. The equity grant provider may have an exit strategy consisting of a 'soft' put option to the original equity investor – 'soft' meaning only when they can finance a full take-over. The grant, thus, becomes a 'conditional grant', comparable to quasi-equity, of which the provider has only lost the inflation (which might be considerable in some of the NAMA host countries), but nevertheless has retained a part of the original grant, which can be reapplied in new investments. The GCF should be ready to resist attempts by the original investor to lower their equity share, in which case the banks would regard the project as even less attractive than had there been no equity grant at all. Applied sensibly, an equity grant could bring some NAMAs that are supported by private sector investments towards financial close.

Otherwise, the GCF, or its peers, should exploit their preferential position in terms of providing 'public equity'. Public equity could be established through the investment in the development of framework conditions. The GCF 'equity' investments could be framed as 'regulatory regime stabilization investments'. The GCF could be a 'sleeping partner' in, for instance, a transmission company responsible for paying out agreed feed-in tariffs. In such a case, its participation would enhance the transmission company's standing in any risk assessment of power purchase agreements with independent power producers, thus, effectively reducing the risk premium, the cost of finance and ultimately the tariff paid for the power. The GCF, as a shareholder, would have a shareholders' agreement with a rather unusual formulation that requires the transmission company to pay out a 105 per cent dividend to the GCF of any saved feed-in tariffs, compared to a benchmark with no GCF 'stabilization'. Similar models could be devised for any NAMA that requires its incremental cost to be paid out as a continuous cash flow from a public sector regulator. The model could be combined with a mixed credit financing arrangement.

The same model is even more attractive, when high upfront costs are outsourced to private sector investments which are profitable over time, like most energy efficiency investments. Funds that address this financing shortfall can be established as revolving funds that return the longer term profits into new investments. This is the fundamental principle in Energy Service

Companies (ESCOs) that overtake the energy supply from, e.g. an inefficient public power producer, activate their capital for investments in efficient equipment, and operate the energy supply over, for instance, a few year period to recover the investment through savings – returning the more efficient energy supply system to the public producer. A 'stabilization' investment may bolster the ESCO's confidence that payments under the contract are safe, despite the obvious significant reduction of operational costs during the contract period – which is the whole idea in the ESCO model – and, thus, a possible public pressure to distribute the savings. Of course, the GCF with its sovereign backing would have to be willing to enforce the integrity of such contracts, if need be. The ESCO model is also used, so far with less success, in the housing sector, where public sector housing could be an object for efficiency investments. They are also conceivable in other contexts where there is a cost of a public service, e.g. in water companies and waste collection companies (waste minimization). The advantage of these investments, compared to, e.g. renewable energy assets, is that the cost of the assets can be accommodated by current cash flows in the sector, and does not need additional and secured cash flow to make the financing come together.

The first recorded moves by the GCF, however, are less visionary. The growing rhetoric that sees the larger share of climate finance stemming from the private sector has increased the pressure on the GCF to position itself accordingly. In this endeavour, however, it has fundamentally misunderstood its role – or it has chosen an easy avenue to appease impatient climate negotiators.

To fast track a private sector window, a subgroup for the Private Sector Facility has been established among the GCF Board's 24 members. While the subgroup may have more in-depth interaction with the private sector, the GCF Board keeps such interactions at a minimum, only occasionally allowing two active observers from civil society organizations and two from private sector organizations, representing developed and developing countries, to participate in the meetings. These may, for instance, be Third World Network and the Sierra Club, representing civil society, and private sector representatives from the Climate Markets & Investment Association (CMIA) and the International Chamber of Commerce. These would not include the banks, the pension funds, the insurance companies, the venture capitalists, and not even the philanthropic foundation trustees. The establishment of one of the central instruments for the financial interaction with the private sector is unfortunately, first and foremost, a public sector undertaking. Its focus must be on financing techniques and financial products – its foundation closer to that of a bank.

The most regrettable consequence of the absence of dialogue between the private sector and the finance community is the establishment of the private sector facility itself. It may be that its establishment is a skilful response to the justifiable impatience among climate negotiators to show progress on the GCF implementation, and not a sign of the prime focus of the GCF. Nevertheless, it is redundant. There are many hybrid finance institutions that are fulfilling this role, with a 30-year track record or more. The GCF is a multilateral institution with the most solidly developed country governments behind it, and a triple A+ rating in its DNA. With this standing, the GCF is to mobilize and maximize private climate investments, not participate in them. If the GCF is intended to become the main instrument for (public) climate funding, and the private sector is expected to deliver anywhere between 50 and 90 per cent of the global climate finance, its mode of collaboration with the most important counterparty is unfortunate. A similar absence of appropriate stakeholder consultation led to the downfall of the CDM.

The Green Climate Fund as Aggregator

The GCF could conceivably be permitted to receive applications, not for finance, but for the financial engineering of a NAMA. In that way, the GCF would avoid having to establish fixed financing schemes – inevitably modelled after existing modes of applying public finance and, thus, not innovating, but simply providing more of the same. With no shortage of funds in the market, more of the same will not bring any projects into materialization that would not have materialized otherwise.

The above ideas are only a few new possible instruments that do not exist as yet. Dozens of others do, however, and they are distributed among hundreds or thousands of financing institutions that may have a role to pay in the financial engineering for NAMAs – or, more correctly, may deploy their for-profit financing capacities if the investment conditions are right. It may, therefore, be that one of the most important potential roles for the GCF is that of the aggregator. Alternatively, the GCF could see it as one of its prime objectives to establish a network of aggregators, licensed or not, to assist in the aggregation of funds and funders in NAMA financing structures. Leaving this job to the NAMA host countries is irresponsible; leaving it to the donors with their track record of donor coordination, despite addressing the shortfalls through the Paris Declaration on Aid Effectiveness, is likely not the optimal solution either. Ruling both out is due to the need for understanding – and accepting – the financing rules of the private sector. It is not helpful for an aggregator, if its approach is the private sector's 'insufficient understanding of sustainability issues', or that the private sector ought to understand that it cannot have its conditions fulfilled. That approach will leave the donors and the NAMA hosts to their own devices.

The aggregators need to understand the points of departure, which are far too often opposing. First and foremost, it will need to align them with the financial engineering of a NAMA that engages all elements necessary, and identifies the financing partners with specific interests in a particular mode of intervention. If the aggregator has financial means at its disposal, like the GCF or other climate finance (donor) programmes, and has the relative freedom to apply financial means adaptable to gaps in the financial engineering of a NAMA, it could have its advantages – but also its disadvantages. Administering a financial supermarket that applies funding on the basis of models that are developed case by case is challenging. It is very expensive to administer, and difficult to market. It is also particularly difficult to justify in terms of 'distributive fairness', which is an issue in climate negotiations that has (too) much attention. When the CDM was established, one of the main concerns raised by G77 and China was exactly how to ensure the distributive fairness of a market-based bottom-up mechanism. It is clearly impossible (but was, nevertheless, addressed by the Nairobi Framework).

The alternative, however, need not be so bad. A network of aggregators, e.g., the hybrid financing institutions, drawing on a widespread network of financing partners and interacting directly with the contributing countries' treasuries – or more likely their development assistance organizations – has all the devices to match the identified needs with identifiable sources of funds and relevant deployment modalities. The GCF would be the obvious centre, if not for management, then to the extent possible for coordination, synergies, concept diffusion and the occasional dollar to bridge the financing of a ground-breaking NAMA. That dollar should be injected as far up in the financing value chain as possible – as discussed at length – at the insurance or even reinsurance level, if feasible. However, this is not only idealized, it is most likely also unrealistic. The GCF will be expected to play a significant financing role, if not delivering USD 100 billion annually, then contributing a significant share. It should endeavour to do so in a complementary manner, and avoid duplication of offers already in the market. Below are a few additional options.

Other Options

NAMA host countries may be under interest regimes that are prohibitive for many projects to materialize. International lending at lower interests may be attractive, but international lenders very rarely offer loans in local currency. Venturing into loans in foreign currency exposes project sponsors to currency fluctuations the cost of which over time should equal out – or exceed – the savings on the interest. The currency risk was one of the main reasons for the demise of the Asian private infrastructure market in the 1990s. Currency risks can be hedged, but in small countries with little foreign trade, the options for taking opposite currency positions are few. The GCF could decide to offer loans in local currency at interest rates comparable to the international interest levels. Canada's Climate Fund established with the Inter-American Development Bank makes up to half of its capital available for loans and guarantees in local currency. Unhedged currency risks, however, become a de facto out-of-pocket expense for the loan provider – unless local interest rates are charged (and then, it may still be). However, the GCF, like the Canadian Fund, could decide that part of its funds should be lost in the currency markets – if this translates into providing access to local affordable financing for NAMAs.

There are other options for the design of loan conditions that better reflect the market exposure of a given project. The Agence Française de Developpement (AFD), for instance, also offers loans with margins indexed on the borrower's performance in terms of social and environmental responsibility, or loans with debt service indexed on raw materials prices.[3] Such options are a mixture of debt service relief and risk mitigation. The Energy Sector Management Assistance Program (ESMAP) has experimented with results-based financing (RBF) that could be relevant in developing countries to promote energy efficiency investments. The fundamental idea of RBF approaches is that 'payments that would otherwise be made automatically are made contingent on delivery of a pre-agreed (set of) result(s), with achievement of the result(s) being subject to independent verification.'[4] The idea is that finance is released only upon achievement of certain pre-specified results. The model is essentially emulating all the ills of the CDM and is a deterrent to private sector investment. It would only be relevant for financing if it could be organized through models like performance bonds, but it brings no benefits to the table for the typical public sector NAMA host. A prudent NAMA hosting government who enters a contract with a private sector company for the delivery of a service would quite naturally use a results-based payment principle. The investment in the delivery system would have been outsourced to the private sector entity, which would have established its investment and financing model to be able to enter the contract. In that respect, results-based finance – implying that a financing plan for a certain activity can be in jeopardy if the private company does not perform according to specifications – would only lead to potential bankruptcy, which would be in neither of the parties' interest. Interim bridge financing needs to be established, and a bridge financier will have to believe, more so than the results-based financier who seems not to believe, in the ability of the private investor to deliver the results. A separate issue is the evaluation of the result, which is where the CDM system failed in securing the carbon asset. The unissued CER is constantly in jeopardy, due to the ex-post evaluation and payment, which are made only upon a third party's evaluation of the performance.

The RBF is meant for the public sector; however, public sector entities are in no better position to accommodate delayed or revoked financing if results, despite efforts to the contrary, are not achieved. A financing model, regardless of whether it is private or public, cannot be based on conditional financing. Only when the entire financing structure is tied up should a NAMA developer push the button. Therefore, it is unlikely that the GCF would be able to leverage any financing for NAMAs through an RBF model.

Instead, inspiration may be sought in 'PEBBLE' structures – the purpose of which is to facilitate patient equity-like capital in greenfield investments. PEBBLE (Pan European Bank to Bond Loan Equitization) has been devised with a distinct European focus and an objective to attract 'patient equity' from global pension funds. But PEBBLEs are in fact loan structures that help lenders adopt different roles depending on their investment horizon and appetite for risk. They offer voting power to the lenders as if they were equity holders[5], introducing first loss ('junior' or 'subordinated') loans that are repaid with a shorter tenor (8 to 10 years) before the long-term senior principal is repaid – designed for institutional investment. PEBBLEs may soften the demand for 'real' equity and provide comfort to lenders and guarantors alike. They may also offer an opportunity for other financing partners such as the ECAs to bridge the first-loss risk cover gap.

The GCF, or any other NAMA financing instrument, might be the source of financing for the development of national emissions trading systems, but only in the role of a grant or loan administrator. It has no role to play as a buyer of carbon credits – unless such purchase agreements are formulated as a performance-based loan. In that case, issuance of a carbon credit is an unnecessary complication, as the credit is developed for a market, not as a measure for loan repayment. A simple measurement of the emissions reduction would do. There is no reason for the GCF to become a party to national carbon trading schemes, unless the GCF in time could see itself as a potential clearing central for the linkage of different national carbon markets. Such a linkage could include 'exchange rates' between different shades of carbon credits to the extent that markets would not accept different levels of stringency applied in different national carbon markets. This kind of function, however, would be much more relevant for established trading platforms.

Instead, the GCF could adopt the principles suggested for a reverse engineering of the CDM, issuing guarantees for the emissions reduction performance of assets, for which there is a statistical basis. Such performance

Figure 18. Options for financial product development

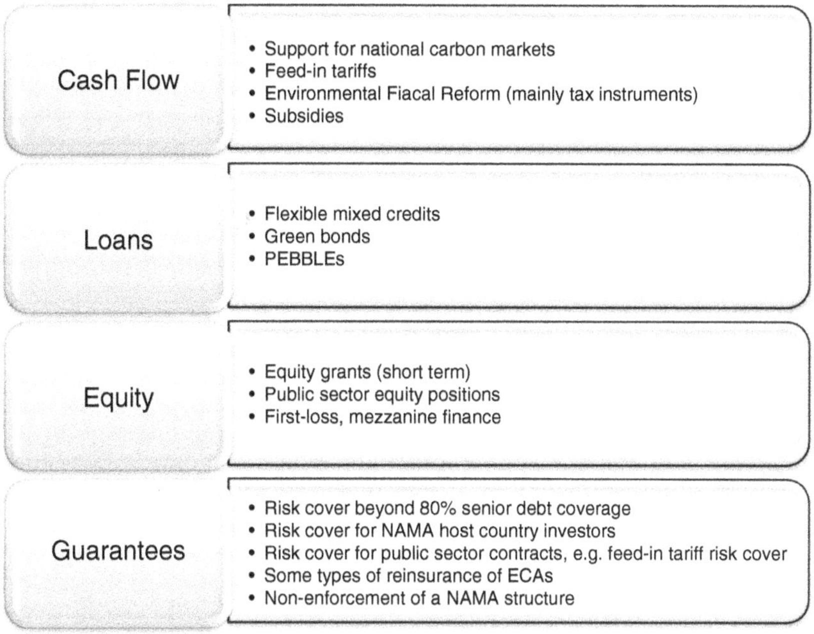

Cash Flow	• Support for national carbon markets • Feed-in tariffs • Environmental Fiacal Reform (mainly tax instruments) • Subsidies
Loans	• Flexible mixed credits • Green bonds • PEBBLEs
Equity	• Equity grants (short term) • Public sector equity positions • First-loss, mezzanine finance
Guarantees	• Risk cover beyond 80% senior debt coverage • Risk cover for NAMA host country investors • Risk cover for public sector contracts, e.g. feed-in tariff risk cover • Some types of reinsurance of ECAs • Non-enforcement of a NAMA structure

guarantees would relate to the establishment of local carbon markets in NAMA host countries, as an instrument to generate cash flows related to emissions reduction. The GCF guarantee would not be based on the issuance of national emissions reduction certificates, as the GCF has neither the authority, nor should it have any interest in issuing certificates without the backing of a real reduction of emissions. Thus, the guarantee would be in the form of a cash-based compensation for the reduction not achieved. Obviously, such a guarantee would not come for free. A similar offer from the GCF could be directed towards the voluntary carbon market, where sellers of VERs take out a guarantee from the GCF to compensate for any shortfall of VER issuance and, thus, less payment from the buyers of the VERs.

Putting the Pieces Together

NAMAs are dynamic instruments that may develop over time, include several elements, involve diverse stakeholders and thrive on a multitude of financing sources. NAMA financing has been defined as the injection of finance into the financing value chain so as to leverage financing on market based terms. Such injections can be in the form of below market interest rates, feed-in tariffs, tax holidays, subsidies, long maturities on loans and not least guarantees in different forms. When designing a financing model for a NAMA, the applicability of instruments as far up in the financing value chain as possible must be explored first. A typical first question, therefore, would be if there is any option for support through the provision of a guarantee model. Such guarantees may be directed at different stakeholders depending on the relevant cash flows. Guarantees may reduce financing costs within certain limits. If further support is needed, the next target would be options for supporting the financing. Equally good would be support of changing cash flows following the implementation of the NAMA. And so forth. Most NAMAs will need to include a number of instruments, to optimize the finance. However, NAMA financing is not the financing of the entire investment – be it a policy, a programme, or a single project.

Ultimately, NAMA financing may be regarded as grants applied in very diverse forms, but a fully grant financed transformational NAMA is simply a contradiction in terms. The most important quality of a NAMA is its ability to change preferences in a sector through alteration of existing cash flows. When looking for options for injection of NAMA finance, it is done relative to an overview of current cash flows. Mapping these cash flows is therefore an important exercise, which can be done with the assistance of the CPEIR and PEER tools. These cash flows originate partly from the national budget, partly from the economic actors in the sector.

In this context, differentiation has been made between climate finance and NAMA finance. Neither have an official definition, but climate finance is commonly regarded as the entire financing that has some kind of relation to climate change. NAMA finance is used more specifically for leveraging, ultimately aiming at leveraging climate finance, but refraining from engaging in large scale asset financing. Figure 18 presents some of the ideas that have been mentioned over the previous pages as options for the engagement of the Green Climate Fund – or other NAMA financiers. It is meant for inspiration only.

Summing Up

The Green Climate Fund is likely to become an important player in NAMA financing. However, it is unlikely that it would be the only provider of NAMA finance, and even more unlikely that it would gather large amounts of capital under the USD 100 billion target. The GCF should avoid redundancy when considering targets for its financing and leveraging capacity. It is in an optimal position for the provision of guarantees for private businesses in NAMA host countries – or possibly guarantees for the public sector when privatizing public utilities – due to its obvious standing, which allows it to exercise its influence towards a NAMA host country that breaches its contracts. The GCF will, but need not, be a financial supermarket. It could benefit from collaborating closely with other relevant public sector financiers, and enhance other agents' effective provision of NAMA finance, while at the same time benefiting from their expertise. The bottom line is that there are gaps that need to be filled, and the Green Climate Fund should see it as its prerogative and purpose, through the filling of these gaps, to leverage NAMA finance.

Chapter 10

CONCLUSION

The NAMA holds the promise of allowing the emissions reduction to be the co-benefit of other worthy initiatives without forgoing the chances of attracting finance that is motivated by the emissions reduction effect. Most actions will therefore be motivated by other concerns – which would perhaps leave them as 'high hanging fruits' in emissions reduction terms. But the NAMA, contrary to the CDM, does not have a specific cost efficiency objective with a focus on reducing one ton of carbon emission in the cheapest way possible. The CDM tried, and failed. The NAMA will not fail on that account, allowing the high hanging fruits to be worthy initiatives that may attract climate-related financing and benefit from either existing instruments, or those that could be added to the toolbox as illustrated in the previous chapters.

Thus far, NAMAs have avoided the discussion of additionality. Even though it requires a deviation from a baseline scenario the effect of this avoidance is likely to promote a wave of 'NAMAfication' of already existing policies and practices. Some NAMAs may therefore not be much other than a labelling exercise. Such NAMAs will ultimately stand the test of appropriateness, not only in their host countries, but among those that are asked to finance them.

The transformational change that bilateral and multilateral donors are expecting from the NAMA is tightly linked to the financial engineering behind it. Although such a change can be achieved by a single investment, a permanent change in cash flows in an economic sector will be the origin of most transformational changes.

The entire exercise in the financial engineering has a double purpose. The first is to reduce the cost of a desirable initiative. The second is to promote that the largest possible share of the financing is provided by the existing financial system with known financial products and known agents. The starting point will always be the current financial flows in a given NAMA host sector and a determination to alter it. It is from here the financial engineering can begin – and where the design of the NAMA starts.

Such changes set certain requirements for the identity of the NAMA proposer. The institutional setting of a 'NAMA development system' in a NAMA host country has not been discussed and is an entirely different subject – and yet the two are linked. Transformational changes in cash flows, increasing some and maybe reducing others, are rarely for a line ministry to initiate on its own. It typically requires the endorsement first and foremost of the Ministry of Finance. Such changes affect stakeholders and challenge vested interests – another discipline that has not been addressed in this context. The financial engineering, therefore, is only one element in the entire NAMA strategy, albeit a central one.

The traditional lesson from project development also goes for the NAMA. The finance sector will always claim that there is plenty of finance for deployment, but a lack of projects. Project developers will claim the opposite. Both are of course right – they simply have not agreed on a common understanding of risk. There *is* sufficient capital for deployment, even local capital as was witnessed by the CDM. However, there is a shortage of models that can activate these funds in contexts that are less than ideal for purposes with emissions reduction benefits. There is a lack of instruments that can address the investment barriers posed by the regulatory systems in NAMA host countries. Some of these instruments have been discussed in this book – the green bond, the equity grant, and the concessional loans – and in particular the focus has been on existing, and especially so far non-existing guarantee products like, e.g., guarantees that would comfort the public sector in dealing with private suppliers of public services. A subset of the guarantee instruments would be directed at improving the quality of the cash flows.

Guarantees should only be offered by those who have the necessary backing to produce their claim in case of default. If a NAMA based on a government administered cash flow (the origin of which may be a donor or multilateral finance institution) defaults on the part the NAMA host government – the guarantee would be called, the guarantor paying out the insurance and the guarantor, possibly with the backing of its government, producing the claim against the defaulting government. Few institutions would have sufficient leverage to reclaim the loss, leaving very few relevant guarantors in the market. In addition to the well-established national export credit agencies and guarantee instruments offered by the multilateral development banks and MIGA, the Green Climate Fund could play a central role, possibly in partnership with the ECAs. If the NAMA host country is a less developed country where a significant share of the government budget stems from bilateral or multilateral assistance the guarantor would have to consider how to administer a preferred creditor position. Calling the guarantee would mean that the traditional assistance would need to cover the loss, effectively shifting funding from development to climate. Therefore, such models are unlikely, supporting the expectation that NAMAs will emerge predominantly in more developed and transition economies. Less developed potential NAMA hosts will focus on Project NAMAs.

Otherwise, Policy NAMAs that introduce permanent changes in cash flows are expected to dominate. Such changes must be dependable if the private sector is to engage. Many instruments seem to have the underlying assumption that the objective is to activate the international private investor and that the bulk of the targeted USD100 billion per year by 2020 will stem from these international private investors. However, it is not spelled out that such considerable participation of international private finance is unlikely to happen before the three other sources have been activated in the order of optimal leveraging: local public budget, international public financing and local private investors.

In a time of financial crisis developing countries are justified in their concern about the dependability of the financial flow of USD 100 billion annually into activities and geographical destinations that are more or less foreign to the majority of international investors. There have been bold ideas of channelling proceeds from the auctioning of emission allowances to the European power sector into the GCF or charging a levy on international sea or air transport. Wherever contributors to the GCF will raise the funds it is unlikely to become a part of the Fund structure. The GCF may therefore well end up suffering from the same replenishment challenges as the GEF and the smaller funds it administers. Funds emerge from rounds of pledges in the traditional UN mode of operation, because donor countries cannot administer a constant outflow of operational budget. COP17 asked the Board to expeditiously establish the policies and procedures to enable an early and adequate replenishment process, making replenishment contingent upon the operationalization of the GCF. However, few, if any, attempts to follow the suggestions by the Secretary-General's High-level Advisory Group on Climate Change Financing[1] have been seen – with the exception of the European Union, although even in Europe the progressive 2011 intercontinental air travel carbon tax was put on hold until April 2014.

It is not difficult to imagine future rescue attempts for a GCF desperately lacking the funds it needs to meet demands from disappointed applicant countries, and in its absence refocusing the GCF funding activities towards lower cost preparation work rather than implementation of actions. To avoid such a potential scenario, the financial instruments adopted or devised by the Board must already, from the start, look at possible partnerships with other financiers to expand the reach of its possibly scarce resources while addressing the challenges in raising real (new) money for this new fund structure. The answer does not lie in numerous bilateral or multilateral donor institutions establishing NAMA financing initiatives and facilities in which they offer a multitude of products that are already in the market, possibly offered by more specialized agencies. Moreover, they may do so in competition for the same clients and on the basis of less than optimal experience in operating such diversity of instruments. Offering loans, subordinated loans, equity and guarantees in one small financial institution may seem efficient from the outside, but it will be difficult and expensive to operate, requiring the accumulation of expertise in all conceivable fields of finance. Offering the same products in a large organization like the GCF might also be problematic, calling for bureaucratic systems to evaluate the different instruments and their applicability in all possible situations.

Instead, the proposed aggregator is likely the answer. Aggregators will have to navigate these waters in search of the NAMA finance based on the financing models that they devise in collaboration with NAMA hosts. The identity of the aggregator may be diverse in the sense that there can be many different models for their establishment. They could emerge in response to a rapidly growing demand among NAMA developers that realize that the starting point for the development of their NAMA is the financial engineering. Alternatively, they could be established as a more top-down driven process in which the international regulatory system – the COP – decides on their formal establishment, just as they did on the establishment of Designated Operational Entities (DOEs) under the CDM. Whichever the route – even if the model would be to engage the GCF in a central aggregation role – the aggregator is needed.

Finally, a piece of speculation. The identity of the NAMA host countries has not been discussed at length though it has been indicated that the ability to create transformational changes through an alteration of a current cash flow will predominantly be something that can be pursued by the more advanced developing countries. Less advanced countries, even Least Developed Countries, are likely left with the 'Project NAMA' option, perhaps even in a CDM-like set-up where the project is isolated from the surroundings through boundary definitions and third party MRV systems. If there is a 'lower cut' in terms of a likely ability to instigate such transformational changes, is there also an 'upper cut'? If so, what constitutes the qualities of the upper cut? Many transition economies may be caught in the middle income trap early on in the life of the NAMA concept. These countries may have difficulties in attracting bilateral or multilateral assistance for the financial engineering of NAMAs, their economies having long graduated from development assistance in the form of grants. On the one hand these are the NAMA host countries that have, by far, the best chances of creating such transformational changes driven by an alteration of the cash flows in a given NAMA host sector. Not only is this because they have a relatively dependable regulatory system, but also because there might already be considerable financial flows for a leveraging exercise to be efficient. But would they be attractive destinations for developed country public NAMA financing? That remains to be seen – but there is a risk that the countries with the best NAMA conditions may occasionally have difficulties raising international public financing. They may in fact have a better chance of raising international private financing. Where would that financing come from? Not necessarily developed countries. The growth in international trade is increasingly made up by growth in South–South trade. It is conceivable that NAMA financing, particularly of the private kind, will follow the same path. Perhaps the financial engineering of NAMAs is ultimately not a North–South exercise with a centrally positioned GCF that administers the North–South divide, but instead a nationally driven NAMA development process that brings in a multitude of financial actors – with the developing countries' own finance in a central role.

How to Start?

If the previous chapters have not answered that question clearly, it is because it is not clear. NAMAs are still in their infancy; the financial engineering of NAMAs even more so. Donors and host countries have commonly embarked on a train that is headed in the right direction, but the stations on the way are less obvious. Not only will host countries have to rethink their current ways of administering budgets in emission prone sectors, but donors will also need to rethink their intervention models to become more demand driven (not in substance, but in funds application mode) and generally more flexible, more concerted and perhaps less afraid to get their hands dirty. But none of this answers the question of how to start.

An overall challenge in providing advice on how to start is that the NAMA is very diverse. It is no longer only emissions reduction initiatives; it is also, and predominantly, initiatives where the emissions reduction is a co-benefit to national agendas with other prime purposes. It pertains to virtually all economic sectors and nearly any kind of implementation model – although in this context, it has been emphasized that not all implementation models are equally beneficial in support of transformational changes. With good reason, the 'official' guidance is vague on strategies for the establishment of an institutional infrastructure for the generation and prioritization of NAMA ideas avoiding to elevate the emissions reduction objective to a prominence that is not justified by the national development priorities – and if NAMA host countries should start by establishing their institutional infrastructure they would never get to the point where they begin embarking on the actual development of NAMAs. And that development process will inevitably require a lot of learning by doing. The best advice, therefore, is probably: just get started.

NOTES

Chapter 1   Introduction

1 Measured on Hawai. The last time atmospheric concentrations of CO_2 were at the same level was 3 million years ago when there was no ice on the poles.
2 See, e.g., the WWF report 'EU Consumption, Global Pollution', January 2008.

Chapter 2   Climate Change and Nationally Appropriate Mitigation Action

1 Article 4 of the United Nation's Framework Convention on Climate Change defines the commitments of all Parties to address greenhouse gas (GHG) emission. The Article states that all Parties, 'taking into account their common but differentiated responsibilities and their specific national and regional development priorities, objectives and circumstances [shall] formulate, implement, publish and regularly update national and, where appropriate, regional programmes containing measures to mitigate climate change by addressing anthropogenic emissions by sources and removals by sinks of all greenhouse gases not controlled by the Montreal Protocol'.
2 http://www4.unfccc.int/sites/nama/SitePages/Home.aspx.
3 See http://www.thegef.org/gef/TT_tech_needs_assessment.
4 Kenneth Baynes, 'Kant on Property Rights and the Social Contract', *The Monist* 72 (3) 1989, 445.
5 The following types of activities may comply with the Gold Standard requirements: renewable energy, energy efficiency, waste handling and disposal if supplying an energy service or a usable product, as well as land use and forests.
6 http://www.international-climate-initiative.com/en/issues/nama-facility/ (accessed 16 June 2013).

Chapter 3   Learning from the CDM

1 PointCarbon, 'Update to Our CER Price Forecast: Phoenix or Dying Swan?' 7 January 2013.
2 The Commission itself said it reacted to a 2 billion allowances surplus in the market. See http://ec.europa.eu/clima/policies/ets/reform/index_en.htm.
3 Data retrieved and processed in April 2013 from the CDMpipeline.org developed by UNEP Risø.

4 Canada and Japan echoed this concern at COP7 saying that 'investor certainty' and 'reducing investor risk' for JI and CDM, was regarded as paramount over and above accountability and environmental assessment. See Y. S. Loong, 'Weather Report from COP7: Calm before the Storm', Third World Network, http://www.twnside.org.sg/title/cop7.htm.

5 FCCC/KP/CMP/2006/10/Add.1, section IV.

6 Based on information from applications under the CDM Loan Scheme.

7 Data from UNEP Risø's PoApipeline shows that only 144,000 CERs have been issued from PoAs compared to 1,419,000,000 CERs from traditional CDM projects. See http://cdmpipeline.org/publications/PoAPipeline.xlsx (accessed 10 February 2014).

8 See http://cdmpipeline.org/ published by UNEP Risø.

9 The author was posted as the Danish Government's representative for purchasing CERs from Chinese CDM projects in that period.

10 See https://www.thepmr.org/.

11 See Michael Lazarus, https://www.thepmr.org/system/files/documents/General%20 Observations%20on%20Crediting%20Mechanisms.pdf.

Chapter 4   Defining NAMA Finance

1 GEF, 2011, http://www.thegef.org/gef/policy/incremental_costs.

2 Banks do, of course, calculate a certain percentage of losses into their interest margin.

3 Basel III is part of the continuous effort made by the Basel Committee on Banking Supervision to enhance the banking regulatory framework. The first version of Basel III was published in late 2009, giving banks about three years to comply with all requirements. Largely in response to the credit crisis, banks are required to maintain proper leverage ratios and meet certain capital requirements. It seeks to improve the banking sector's ability to deal with financial and economic stress and improve risk management. Excerpts from http://www.investopedia.com/terms/b/basell-iii.asp (accessed 2 June 2013).

4 'We need one of those too...'

5 This is elaborately discussed in S. E. Lütken and A. Michaelowa, 'Corporate Strategies and the CDM – Developing Country Financing for Developed Country Commitments', 2008.

6 'Unburnable carbon' refers to the fact that only a third of the world's know fossil fuel reserves can be burnt if global average temperature increases are to stay below 2 degrees Celsius (International Energy Agency, 2012).

Chapter 5   The Financing Tools . . .

1 For a recent example of a suggestion of EFR, see 'Summary for Policy-Makers. Green Revenues for Green Energy: Environmental Fiscal Reform for Renewable Energy Technology Deployment in China', IISD & China National Renewable Energy Centre, (c) October 2013.

2 A good overview of Indian policy incentives can be found at http://www.spartastrategy.com/blog/2011/07/your-incentives-road-map-for-the-indian-energy-sector/, also listing the following instruments employed:
   • 100 per cent accelerated depreciation in the first year of the installation of projects and systems;

- Low import tariffs for capital equipment and most of the materials and components;
- Soft loans to manufacturers and users for commercial and near commercial technologies;
- Five-year tax holiday for power generation projects;
- Facility for banking and wheeling of power.

3 Climate-l, 22 January 2013 and http://climatepolicyinitiative.org/publication/risk-gaps/.
4 See http://www.thepmr.org/.
5 The EU Emission Trading System (ETS) showed the way by fining non-delivery of the offset against commitments with EUR 100 per tCO_2e.

Chapter 6   . . . And the Financiers

1 GCF/B.01-12/04, http://gcfund.net/fileadmin/00_customer/documents/pdf/B.01-12.04_Work_plan_of_the_Board_FINAL.pdf.
2 See http://gcfund.net/home.html.
3 See http://nama-facility.org/projects/projects-selected.html.
4 With four key programmes helping 48 developing countries pilot low emissions and climate resilient development: Clean Technology Fund (CTF), Pilot Program Climate Resilience (PPCR), Forest Investment Program (FIP) and Scaling Up Renewable Energy Program (SREP).
5 See http://www.iigcc.org/__data/assets/pdf_file/0020/15383/Global-investor-survey-on-climate-change-Final.pdf.
6 International Strategy for Disaster Reduction, 2010, http://cred.be/sites/default/files/PressConference2010.pdf.
7 A full list is available on EKFs website, http://www.ekf.dk/en/WhatWeDo/Products/Pages/default.aspx.
8 For an overview of the European development finance institutions, including the well-known German KFW, see www.edfi.eu.
9 http://www.scaf-energy.org/.
10 See http://climatebonds.net/.
11 See, e.g., http://www.ceres.org/resources/reports/green-bond-principles-2014-voluntary-process-guidelines-for-issuing-green-bonds.
12 http://climatebonds.net/wp-content/uploads/2012/05/CB-HSBC_Final_30May12-A3.pdf.
13 At a NAMA Financing conference in Copenhagen in May 2013.

Chapter 8   Challenges to NAMA Finance – Mandates, Aggregation and Lack of Instruments

1 http://stats.oecd.org/glossary/detail.asp?ID=5974.
2 See the Climate Policy Initiative's 'Mapping the World Bank Group Risk Mitigation Instruments for Climate Change', at http://climatepolicyinitiative.org/wp-content/uploads/2013/09/World-Bank-Group-Risk-Mitigation-Instruments-for-Climate-Change-Brief1.pdf.
3 See the latest revision of the mandates (consensus rules) for the Export Credit Agencies, http://www.oecd.org/tad/xcred/theexportcreditsarrangementtext.htm.

Chapter 9   Roles of the Green Climate Fund

1 'Quasi-sovereign' is not a fixed term or definition, but refers to situations where – despite a government guarantee – a risk still remains, either by specific exemption, or because the sovereign guarantee is provided by a government with limited capacity to honour such guarantees. ECAs can guarantee such sovereign guarantees – called 'MoF guarantees', but they do so only because they have sovereign leverage, i.e., backing from their host government. If the Ministry of Finance at the investment destination does not honour its obligation as a guarantor, it becomes an inter-governmental matter.
2 E.g., a 30 per cent uncovered tranche and a 70 per cent tranche guaranteed by the ECA. The market would then determine the price on both, and buyers would choose on the basis of their appetite for risk.
3 http://www.afd.fr/lang/en/home/outils-de-financement-du-developpement/prets.
4 http://www.esmap.org/node/2866.
5 Which many lenders would not appreciate as it gives them a double position of lenders and equity holders leaving, them with a potential conflict of interests.

Chapter 10   Conclusion

1 See 'Report of the Secretary-General's High-level Advisory Group on Climate Change Financing', http://www.un.org/wcm/webdav/site/climatechange/shared/Documents/AGF_reports/AGF%20Report.pdf.

REFERENCES

Caravani A., S. Nakhooda, C. Watson, L. Schalatek. 2012. *The Global Climate Finance Architecture*. ODI and Heinrich Böll Stiftung, November 2012.

Climate Bonds Initiative (CBI). 2013. 'Bonds and Climate Change: The State of the Market in 2013'. http://www.climatebonds.net/wp-content/uploads/2013/08/Bonds_Climate_Change_2013_A4.pdf.

Climate Policy Initiative. 2012. 'The Landscape of Climate Finance 2012'. Barbara Buchner, Angela Falconer, Morgan Hervé-Mignucci, Chiara Trabacchi.

_____. 2013. 'Risk Gaps: A Map of Risk Mitigation Instruments for Clean Investments'. Gianleo Frisari, Morgan Hervé-Mignucci, Valerio Micale, Federico Mazza.

Development Assistance Committee (DAC). 2011. '2011 DAC Report on Multilateral Aid'. OECD.

Global Environment Facility (GEF). 2012. 'Report of the Global Environment Facility to the Eighteenth Session of the Conference of the Parties to the United Nations Framework Convention on Climate Change'. FCCC/CP/2012/6.

GEF/UNEP Risø. 2012. 'Accessing International Financing for Climate Change Mitigation, 2012'.

International Energy Agency (IEA). 2012. 'World Energy Outlook 2012'.

Kirkman, G. A., E. Haites, S. Seres, R. Spalding-Fecher. 2012. 'Benefits of the Clean Development Mechanism'. UNFCCC. http://cdm.unfccc.int/about/dev_ben/index.html.

Lawson, Bird. 2008. 'Environmental Funding: How to Increase the Effectiveness of Public Expenditure in Developing Countries', Summary Report. http://www.odi.org.uk/publications/2982-environmental-funding-effectiveness-public-expenditure-developing-countries.

Lütken, S. E. 2005. 'Corporate Strategies and the Applicability of the Clean Development Mechanism pre- and post-2012'. Aalborg University, 2005.

———. 2008. 'Developing Country Financing for Developed Country Commitments?' UNEP Risø Perspectives 2008.

_____. 2011. 'Indexing CDM Distribution – Levelling the Playing Field'. UNEP Risø, Working Paper No. 10.

_____. 2012. 'Penny Wise, Pound Foolish?' UNEP Risø, Working Paper No. 1.

Lütken, S. E. and A. Michaelowa. 2008. *Corporate Strategies and the Clean Development Mechanism*. Cheltenham: Edward Elgar, 2008.

Michaelowa, A. 2012. 'Scenarios for the Global Carbon Markets'. Paper 1 for the CDM Policy Dialogue.

Organisation for Economic Co-operation and Development (OECD). 2011. 'Environmental Outlook to 2050'.

Overseas Development Institute (ODI). 2011. 'Mapping the New Infrastructure Financing Landscape'. Christian K. M. Kingombe, Background Note, April.

Prahalad, C. K., G. Hamel. 1990. 'The Core Competence of the Corporation'. *Harvard Business Review*, May 1990.

Rockefeller Philanthropy Advisors. 2008. 'Philanthropy's New Passing Gear. Mission-Related Investing: A Policy and Implementation Guide for Foundation Trustees'.

Swanson, Lunde. 2003. 'Public Environmental Expenditure Reviews'. World Bank, Environment Department, Environment Strategy Papers. Washington, DC, 2003.

UNDP. 2011. 'Blending Climate Finance through National Climate Funds', September.

UNDP/ODI. 2012. 'The Climate Public Expenditure and Institutional Review (CPEIR): A Methodology to Review Climate Policy, Institutions and Expenditure', August 2012. http://www.odi.org.uk/publications/6191-cpeir-methodology-climate-finance-national-public-expenditure.

UNEP. 2013. 'The Emissions Gap Report 2013 – A Synthesis Report'. http://www.unep.org/publications/ebooks/emissionsgapreport2013/.

UNEP FI. 2012. 'Creating the "New Normal": Enabling the Financial Sector to Work for Sustainable Development'. United Nations Environment Programme Finance Initiative Discussion Paper, October.

UNEP FI/IISD. 2013. 'South-Originating Green Finance: Exploring the Potential', November.

UNEP Risø. 2011. 'Low Carbon Development Strategies: Framing National Appropriate Mitigation Actions (NAMAs) in Developing Countries'.

_____. 2012. 'Measuring Reporting Verifying: A Primer on MRV for Nationally Appropriate Mitigation Actions'.

_____. 2013. 'Understanding the Concept of Nationally Appropriate Mitigation Action'.

UNFCCC. 1992. 'United Nations Framework Convention on Climate Change'.

_____. 'United Nations Framework Convention on Climate Change'. FCCC/CP/2007/6/Add.1/Decision 1/CP.13 Bali Action Plan. http://unfccc.int/resource/docs/2007/cop13/eng/06a01.pdf#page=3. Accessed 4 January 2013.

_____. 'United Nations Framework Convention on Climate Change'. FCCC/CP/2010/7/Add.1/Decision 1/CP.16 Cancun Agreements: Outcome of the Work of the Ad Hoc Working Group on Long-term Cooperative Action under the Convention. http://unfccc.int/resource/docs/2010/cop16/eng/07a01.pdf#page=2.

_____. 2011. 'United Nations Framework Convention on Climate Change'. FCCC/CP/2011/Decision -/CP.17 Outcome of the Work of the Ad Hoc Working Group on Long-term Cooperative Action under the Convention. http://unfccc.int/resource/docs/2011/cop17/eng/09a01.pdf. Accessed 4 January 2013.

_____. 2012a. 'Early Submission of Information to the NAMA Registry Prototype'. http://unfccc.int/cooperation_support/nama/items/6945.php. Accessed 24 November 2012.

_____. 2012b. 'Draft Decision -/CP.18. Agreed Outcome Pursuant to the Bali Action Plan'. http://unfccc.int/files/meetings/doha_nov_2012/decisions/application/pdf/cop18_agreed_outcome.pdf. Accessed 14 February 2013.

UNFCCC/UNDP/UNEP Risø. 2013. 'Guidance for NAMA Design: Building on Country Experiences'. UNDP.

WWF. 2008. 'EU Consumption, Global Pollution', January.

INDEX

Numbers appearing in bold refer to the figure or table on the page.

additionality 15, 27, 33–4, 137; *see also* baselines
African Development Bank 74
African Union Commission (AUC) 69
Agence Française de Developpement (AFD) 131
aggregation gap 102–5
aggregators: candidates for role of 74; central role of 103–4, **104**; drafting financing models 80; ECAs as 109–10; GCF as 129–30; need for 54, 70, 124, 140; role in financing value chain 95–6
American Overseas Private Investment Corporation's (OPIC) 107–8
approval process in CDM 35–6, **36**
'Arrangement on Guidelines for Officially Supported Export Credits' 111
Asian Development Bank 74

Bali Roadmap 9
bank interest 144ch4n2
bankable projects 42, 113, 117
banks 76–7, 108; *see also* development banks
Basel III 42, 144ch4n3
baselines 24, 33–4; *see also* additionality
bilateral aid **95**, **104**; in development planning 19; expectations from 137, 139–40; financial structures of 68; Germany's 69; from grants 79; in NAMA host countries 138; in NAMAs 14; public development finance channelled through 41–2; in risk distribution efforts 120; risk mitigation qualities of 74; from state

budgets 78; for transition economies 140; used to buy CERs 16
Bilateral Offset Crediting Mechanism (Japan) 29, 62
'blend' countries 111
blending financing 79–80
bond market 77
bonds 106, 122; *see also* green bonds
'Bonds and Climate Change' 78
BOT market 118
Brown, Gordon 10
budget analysis 81–2, 94
building sector 109
'buyer's credit insurance' 106

C40 Cities Climate Leadership group 64–5
Canada 144ch3n4
Canada Climate Fund 131
Cancun Agreements (2010) 9–10, 17, 39
cap-and-trade (emissions trading): by bankers 10; NAMA financing role in 132; national vs. international regimes 64; promoting emissions reduction through 37; safeguards 63; schemes in NAMA host countries 24; tax mechanisms for 58
capacity: administrative 23–4; cash flow 80; climate finance 93; GCF addressing shortfalls in 126; GCF's real money injection 84–5; innovative 40, 43; of NAMA hosts financing 93; NAMAs' shortfalls of 79; of profit and non-profit sectors 83
capacity building 2, 9, 31, 39, 89
capital 29, 122–3, 127, 134

capital expenditure 82
carbon assets 35, 85
carbon dioxide 2, 3, 143ch1n1
carbon emission liabilities 72
carbon markets 13; cap-and-trade schemes in NAMA host countries 24; consequences of failure of 77; ECAs in 73; inefficiencies created by 13, 27; national 64; 'one-revenue stream' projects 28, 143ch3n3; PMR shaping next generation of 62; voluntary 47, 133; see also CDMs; CERs
carbon revenues 85
cash flow: alteration of existing 134; determining values and preferences 83; differentiated from investment 54; emissions trading creating 97; enhancement of 61, 65; expanded securitization model of 118, **119**; financing model for increasing 89; grant-based guarantee structures for 114; green bonds enhancing 80; lack of long-term 122; reflecting process 84; subsidies supporting 107; of transformational NAMAs 96, 137–8; voluntary carbon credits providing 63
CDMs. See: Clean Development Mechanisms
Certified Emissions Reductions (CERs): approval of 35–6, **36**; buying 10; cost inefficient emissions reductions 31–3; guarantees for issuance 36; issuance of from PoAs 31, 144n7; jeopardy of unissued 132; limitation of generation capacity 93; managing overhang of 62–3; market influences on 28; positive externality of 28, 32; see also carbon markets
challenges to NAMA finance 101–2; aggregation gap 102–5; consensus standards 113; ECAs as aggregators 109–10; guarantee system and its shortcomings 105–9; mandates 110–15
China 14, 17, 31, 78, 130, 144n9
Clean Development Mechanism Programme Activities (CPAs) 15

Clean Development Mechanism Rulebook 34
Clean Development Mechanisms (CDMs): co-benefits of 43–4; complexity of 25; differences from NAMA 11, 13, 85, 87, 137; distinguishing project activities from NAMAs 11; documentation 28; ex-post approval of 35; goal of 25; household installations distributed by 91; initiatives of 1–2; leveraging in 85; local investment in 89–90, 93; methodological toolbox of 26–7; patterns of investment in 30; profitability perspective of projects 26; reverse engineering 34–7, 96; Rulebook 34; shortcomings of 89, 96; status of in 'climate community' 10–11; vulnerability to market forces 27; see also carbon markets; learning from the Clean Development Mechanism
Clean Technology Fund (CTF) 70, 145n4
climate assistance models 97
Climate Bonds Initiative 77–8, 122
Climate Bonds Standard 125
Climate Change Windows (CCWs) 69
'climate community' 10–11
climate expenditure 82
climate finance 39–41, 51–2, 134
climate finance capacity 93
Climate Finance Project (CPI's) 41
Climate Investment Fund (CIF) 70, 77
Climate Policy Initiative (CPI) 41, 61, 105, 107
Climate Public Expenditure and Institutional Review (CPEIR) 81–2, 134
climate-related ODA funding 69
climate risk 72
co-insurance 107, 120; see also insurance
Common but Differentiated Responsibilities (CBDR) 17
concessional financing: in financing value chain 94, **94**; IDA's 111–13; for Least Developed Countries 77; in loans and guarantees 61–2; in long-term models 97; from NAMA

Facility 69–70; risks addressed by 105; role of 118
Conference of Parties: Cancun (2010) 17, 68; COP17 139; Doha (2012) 25, 68; Nairobi (2005) 30; progress of 10; Warsaw (2013) 11; *see also* UNFCCC
consulting sector CDM role 10
Copenhagen Accord 21
core business 47, 73, 90, 92, 109
core competencies 90
corporate social responsibility (CSR) 46–7, 71
corporatized public entities 53, 83, 91, 112
cost dictating selection 21
counting emissions 13, 16
country risk 91; *see also* risk
credit insurance 106, 112
crediting model requirements 36
cross-subsidization 23, 57, 87
currency risk 130

debt service 61, 84, 131
defining NAMA finance: business as usual (BAU) scenario 44–5, 54; conflicts of interest 44; definition of climate finance 40; definition of NAMA finance 42–3, 48; financial engineering of NAMAs 43, **44**, 51, 54; financing unprofitable projects 52; government investment motives 44–6; 'incremental cost' approach to climate financing 40–41, 43; 'innovative financing models' 40–41; market rate loans and equity 42; matrix of finance categories 39, 86; private investment motives 46–8, 52; private sector funding 41–2, 51; public–public partnerships 43; total cost approach 43
demand 45
depreciation, variable or accelerated **21**, **55**, 60, 144–5ch5n2
design of NAMAs 11, 24
Deutsche Gesellschaft für Internationale Zusammenarbeit GmbH (GIZ) 69
developed countries: emissions reduction investment by 29; emitter status 2–3; funding models of 114; GCF

mobilized from 10; green bonds 125; Kyoto Protocol impact on 1, 9; negotiation mandates for 39; project inefficiencies in 32; responsibilities of 2
developing countries: Bali Action Plan guidelines for 9; climate change policy in 17; climate finance capacity 93; domestic investment capital in 29–30; emission reductions in 30; emissions reduction investment by 29; emitter status 2–3; energy sectors in 12, 52; key programmes in 145n4; negative private sector experiences of 121; thriving on domestic finance 29; *see also* Least Developed Countries
development application models 97
development assistance administration 114
Development Assistance Committee (DAC) of OECD 113
development banks 67, 74, 76–7, 108, 120; *see also specific institutions*
Development Finance Institutions 53
development objectives 3
development planning 19, **19**, 48; *see also* NAMA development
'distributive fairness' 130
documentation 28, 31
domestic investment capital in developing countries 29–30
drivers 20, 28, 32–3, 44, 47, 63, 91; *see also specific kinds of*
due diligence 71, 74, 77, 108–9
Durban Platform 10

E+ and E- regulations 33–4
economic incentives 13, 21–2; *see also* incentives
'economies of scale' in risk distribution 120
emissions: baseline definition 24; as externality 20; measuring reduction activity 22, 26; negotiation outcomes on 1; outsourcing of 3; shift to developing countries 2
emissions reduction: budgets as source of priorities for 81; co-benefits of 44, 45, 88; determination of 52; in developing countries 30; energy efficiency option 90; fossil fuel

subsidies impacting 60–61; goal of NAMA financiers 88; leveraging carbon revenues 85; sub-optimal investments in 45, **46**
Emissions Reduction Purchase Agreements (ERPA) 31, 36
energy efficiency investments 47, 109, 127, 131
energy sector 52–3, 72, 91
Energy Sector Management Assistance Program (ESMAP) 131
Energy Service Companies (ESCOs) 108–9, 127–8
enforcement systems 12, 14, 22, 63–4, 145ch5n5; *see also* non-enforcement of NAMAs
'Environmental Fiscal Reform' (EFR) **22**, 55–9, 57, 59, 86–7
environmentally friendly activities 78
equity: as climate finance aid 41; in expanded securitization model **119**; as financial product **133**; in financing value chain **95**; GCF and 126–9; guarantees impact on 61; investors **104**, 105; origination of 86; 'patient' 132; in PEBBLEs 132; positions 122; private sector 53, **55**, 65; project example 123; return requirements 92
equity grants **95**, 127, **133**, 138
equity requirements 123
EU-Africa Infrastructure Trust Fund 69–70
European Bank for Reconstruction and Development (EBRD) 53, 74
European Commission 28, 69, 143ch3n2
European Emission Trading System (EU ETS) 28, 63
evaluation criteria 18, 143n5
Export Credit Agencies (ECAs): as aggregator candidate 80; climate bond guarantee by 78; disadvantages of 110; GCF involving 120; grants 113; hybrids using 92; mandates 111–12; private investor use of 91; regulation of 111; roles of 72–3, 101, 105–10, 114, 123–5; shortcomings of 108, 121, 123–4;

uncovered risks 120–21; *see also* hybrid financing; risk
Export Credit Fund (EKF) 73, 112
Export Development Canada (EDC) 73
externalities 20, 25, 28, 34, 55–6
externalities regulated against 55–9, **57**

feed-in tariff insurance 107–8
feed-in tariffs (FiTs) 13, **21**, **55**, 59–60
financial drivers 20–21
financial engineering: altering financial flows 83; for carbon assets 35; cross-subsidization example 23; defined 4; leveraging vs. 81; of NAMAs 43, **44**, 51, 54, 89, 129, 134; objectives of 88, 137; origination of 81; strategies 4; unilateral vs. internationally supported 12, 14; *see also* Green Climate Fund (GCF); NAMA Facility
financiers: banks 76–7; behind NAMA 70; blending 79–80; ECA insured 112; EU-based instrument implementation model 69–70; green bonds 77–80; hybrid sources 74–6, 80, 92, 105, 112, 126; institutional investors 70–72, 78–9; insurance companies 72–4; international 88; overview of 67–8; philanthropic foundation trustees 75–6; refinancing 71; traditional virtues sought by 88; *see also* NAMA Facility
financing tools: cash flow and investment differentiation 54; commitment time frames 63–4; concessional 62; cost of types of risk 62, **63**; enforcement systems for 63, 145ch5n5; fate of carbon credits 62–5; multilateral investment in mitigation and typical instruments employed 53, **53**; non-domestic sources **55**, 59; non-financial 51; overview 21, 51; public sector operational instruments 53–4, 59–65; public sector sourcing instruments 54–9, **55**; sourcing instruments and operational instruments for NAMA financing 94; voluntary carbon credits 63–4

financing value chain **94**, 94–6, 101, 126, 133–4
financing value chain instruments 94–5, **95**
first-loss loans 132
first-loss protection instruments 105, 132
fixed assets 72
Foreign Direct Investment (FDI): in energy sector 83; in leveraging 91–2; NAMA projects lack of 30; risk guarantees for 73; as unrealistic 37
foreign donor intervention 89
Forest Investment Program (FIP) 145n4
fossil-fuel-based energy generation 93

G77 concerns 130
German bilateral assistance programmes 69
German Federal Ministry for the Environment, Nature Conservation and Nuclear Safety 68
Global Environment Facility (GEF) 17, 40–41, 67, 70, 117
global temperature 2
Gold Standard Foundation 18, 64, 143n5
grants 59–60; in blended financing 70; DAC rules on 113; donor activities 89; ECA 113; 'equity grants' 127; in IDA commitments 111; in leveraging 96, 102; role of 97, 118; timing of 79
green bonds 77–80, 114–15, 122–6, **126**, 146n2; see also bonds
Green Climate Fund (GCF) 68; as aggregator 129–30; capitalization of 39, 68; equity and 126–9; establishment of 10; existing markets vs. 117; expanded securitization model of cash flow system 118–21, **119**; expanding existing coverage of ECAs 120; financing role of 130; goal 103; governing instrument 117; green bonds and 122–6, **126**; leveraging role of 84–5; market openings for 88, 122, 124, 127, 131–2, 134–5, 138; options for financial product development 130–34, **133**; position of 128; Private Sector Facility 128; replenishment challenges to 139; and risk 120–22;

Southern African Power Pool 123–4, **124**; 'stabilization' investments 127–8; stakeholder participation 128–9; standardization of climate bonds 125; target market of 118; using CDM's reverse engineering principles 132–3; see also financial engineering
Group on Climate Change 72
guarantee systems: for CERs 35–7; criteria for 138; enhanced 80; grant-based for cash flows 114; importance of 101; loans and 61–2; models 134, 138; shortcomings of 105–9, 115, 121; support of 96; through MIGA 77; see also ECA; insurance; sovereign risk cover
guidelines for green bonds 78

Heinrich Böll Foundation 70
Hermes 73
household installations initiatives 91
housing sector 128
hybrid financing: as aggregator 80, 105; characteristics of 92; equity and 126; as network of aggregators 130; risk in 112; sources of 74–6; see also ECAs
hydrocarbons 1

incentives: example of 23; grants as 60; insufficient 29; in PoAs 16; regulatory 65; sector alteration of 96; World Bank discussions of 33; see also economic incentives
'incremental cost' approach to climate financing 40–41, 51, 60, 67, 103, 119; grant element in 125–6
independent power producers (IPPs) 83
industrial energy efficiency 90
infrastructure: corporatizing of 83; financial engineering of private 103, 119; institutional investors 70–72; multilateral development banks funding 76; risk aversion in 121; scale of projects 78; service demand prediction 84
initiatives, sources of 17
institutional analysis 82

institutional investors 70–72, 78–9,
    114–15, 132
insurance: co-insurance 107, 120;
    companies 72–4; credit 106;
    ECA 107; feed-in tariff 106–7;
    reinsurance 73–4, 98, 107, 120–21;
    role in leveraging NAMA finance
    97–8; self-insurance strategy 124;
    see also guarantees; risk
Inter-American Development Bank 131
internal rate of return (IRR) 33
International Climate Initiative (IKI) 69
International Development Agency
    (IDA) 111
International Finance Corporation (IFC)
    53, 74, 105
International Institute for Sustainable
    Development (IISD) 93
investment climates 29–30
investment drivers: behind CDM projects
    31, 49; in core business 92; crediting
    model requirements 36; emissions as
    28, 43, 49; motivations behind 46;
    traditional externalities as 34

Japan 29, 62, 144ch3n4
Joint Implementation 36

KfW Development Bank 69
KPMG International's Corporate
    Sustainability progress report 47
Kyoto Protocol 1–2, 9

Latin American Investment Facility 69–70
Learning from CDM: additionality 33–4;
    the CDM experience 26–7; cost
    inefficient emissions reductions
    31–3; distribution of carbon returns
    on investment 31, **32**; imbalances
    30–31; market influences 28–9;
    overview 25–6; thriving on domestic
    finance 29–30, 144ch3n4; *see also*
    Clean Development Mechanism
Least Developed Countries 18, 77, 91,
    140; *see also* developing countries
Least Developed Country Fund (LDCF) 70
leveraging finance: in CDMs 85; developed
    country support 93; from different

sources 84–92; domestic public
    funding 86–8; engineering vs.
    81; FDI in 91–2; financing value
    chain 94; focus on 4, 68; with hard
    regulation 97; household financing
    91; international financiers 88;
    intervention option categories and
    relationships 94, **94**; maximizing
    96, 102, 111; mechanism of 40;
    model completion 85; motivations
    considerations 83; NAMA finance
    role of 48, 133–4; 'NAMA financing
    gap' 97; 'new market mechanisms'
    97; parallel provision use 90; private
    sector 84, 89–91; in relation to assets
    94; right order of 92–7, 139; risk
    profiles impacting on 84; sequencing
    of 85–6, **86**; transformation 83–4
Linddal, M. 82
loan models 59, 62, 70
Low Emission Development Strategies
    (LEDS) 17, **19**
Lütken, S. E. 26, 144ch4n5

M1 countries 22–3
mandates 110–15
Marginal Abatement Cost (MAC) curves 26
Marginal Abatement Revenue (MAR) 26, 32
market drivers 25, 27, 32
markets as political constructs 36
Marrakech Accords 26
Measurement, Reporting and Verification
    (MRV): of Policy NAMAs 22
mechanism of NAMAs 11
Mexico 62, 87
Michaelowa, A. 26, 144ch4n5
Ministry of Environment 87–8
Ministry of Finance 82, 89, 113, 124, 138
Ministry of Foreign Affairs 87
Mission Related Investment (MRI) 75–6
mitigation actions 3–4, 12; *see also* NAMAs
mitigation investments 42
mixed credits (soft loans) **55**, 113, 125
mobilizing funding 40
multilateral development banks 76–7,
    95, **104**, 120, 138; *see also specific
    institutions*
multilateral donors 19, 74, 137, 139–40

Multilateral Investment Guarantee Agency (MIGA) 106

Nairobi Framework 30–31
NAMA development 81, 86–7; *see also* development planning
NAMA Facility 14, 23, 68–9, 79, 80, 103; *see also* financial engineering
NAMA host countries: appropriateness determinations by 18–19; interest regimes 130; 'NAMA development systems' in 137–8; need for aggregators 129; regulatory barriers in 138
NAMA Registry 12, 69, 110
NAMAs ('Nationally Appropriate Mitigation Actions'): additionality requirements 33; aligning drivers with 33; appropriateness criteria for 18; characteristics of 133; co-benefits of 44–5, 49; defining appropriateness 16–20; definition of 11, 12; differences from CDM 11, 13, 85, 87, 137; financial engineering of 43, **44**, 51, 54, 89; in general development planning 19, **19**, 48; host countries lacking ECA equivalents 107; identity of 10–15; initiation of 9; international negotiation texts on 39; layered, phased and parallel 23; LEDS as framework of 17; leveraging in 85; miscommunication about 79; 'official' NAMA guidance 81; overview of 3–5; PoAs and 15–16; as policy related 89; 'Policy' vs. 'Project' 12–13, 110; project purposes 27; relevance of 30; substance of 20–24; unilateral vs. internationally supported 12, 14; as vehicle to LEDS 19–20; volatility 45
national appropriateness 18, 20, 103–4
national budgets: analysis of 81–2; appropriations to public investment budgets 54; bolstering 114; central role of 141; incremental cost in 41; NAMA funding from 82, 86; negotiation delegation limitations 87

national capacity to administer MRV systems 22, **22**
National Designated Entities (NDEs) 87
national development banks 77; *see also* development banks
National Development Plans 19
national emissions sectors 87
national investors **63**, 121–2
national public sector 86, 93; *see also* public sector
National Strategic Development Planning 19, **19**
national trading systems 27
negotiations 1, 10
Neighbourhood Investment Facility 69–70
New Market Mechanisms 35
non-enforcement of NAMAs 121, **133**; *see also* enforcement systems
non-profit sector 83

'one-revenue stream' projects 28, 31, 143ch3n3
operational assets 61
operational instruments, 53–4
Organisation for Economic Co-operation and Development (OECD) 73, 91, 101, 113
outsourcing of emissions 3
Overseas Development Institute (ODI) 53, 70, 81–2
ownership structures 83

Paris Declaration on Aid Effectiveness 129
Partnership for Market Readiness (PMR) 35, 62, 64
PEBBLEs (Pan European Bank to Bond Loan Equitization) structures 132
PEER studies 82, 134
philanthropic foundation trustees 75–6
Pilot Program Climate Resilience (PPCR) 145n4
PIN (Project Information Note) 36
policy analysis 82
policy development 101
policy financing models 110
Policy NAMAs: defined 13; expectations for 139; in general development

planning 19, **19**; managing risk 105;
    representing or requiring action 21,
    21; weight of vs. Project NAMAs
    relative to capabilities of developing
    countries **22**, 22–3
policy risk insurance (CPI) 105
policy strategy 87
positive net present values (NPVs) 41
Power Purchase Agreements (PPAs)
    64, 112
preferred creditor positions 138–9
pricing 56
Primer on Low Carbon Development
    Strategies (UNEP Risø 2011) 10
private sector: bank relationship 42; core
    business and initiative alignment
    47; of corporatized public entities
    91; deterrents to 85; engagement
    via securitization model 122; equity
    grants bolstering 127; expanding
    role of 53; financing instruments
    55; funding climate finance 39–41;
    host countries' 93; leveraging finance
    84, 89–91; loans to 62; motives for
    climate friendly investment 46–7,
    144ch4n4; NAMA financing 12,
    89; permanence as priority to 83;
    philanthropy imitating 75; in PoAs
    15–16; result-based financing for 37,
    131–2; role of guarantees with 80;
    small scale climate investments 108;
    view of regulation 90
Private Sector Facility 128
profit sector 43, 83
Programmes of Activity 15–16, 31, 144n7
project approach 23, 110
project development 138
Project NAMAs 13, 14, 19, **19**, 20, 22, **22**
Prototype Carbon Fund 35
public development finance 41–2
'public equity' 127
public sector: in developing countries 52;
    funding of NAMAs 39–40, 86–8;
    gap in risk cover for 121;
    regulation 65
public sector operational instruments
    54, **55**; accelerated depreciation
    60, 144–5ch5n2; feed-in tariffs **55**,

59–60; grants 59–60, 70, 79, 89;
    loans and guarantees 61–2; subsidy
    removal 60–61; taxes 60–61
public sector sourcing instruments **55**;
    direct and indirect taxation 56, **57**;
    environmental fiscal reform 55–9;
    non-domestic sources 59; prices
    on products and services 56; tax
    structure considerations 56–8
public–private partnerships (PPPs) 48;
    collaboration model 118; funding
    NAMAs 65; hybrid 74–6, 80, 92,
    105, 126; improved climate for 53;
    risk aversion in 121; using *sourcing*
    instruments 54
public–public partnerships 40, 43

quasi-equity **95**
'quasi-sovereign' bonds 124, 146ch9n1

reallocation 86–7
recurrent spending 54, 60, 82
refinancing 71
regulatory environment 11, 13
regulatory instruments **21**, 42
regulatory systems: desirable characteristics
    of 90; differentiating instruments
    54; of ECAs 111; for externalities
    20, 46–7, 55–6; forcing change 21,
    107; gold picking imposed by 90;
    international 140. (see also COP);
    sector specific 54; used in leveraging
    97; wording of 14
reinsurance 73–4, 98, 107, 120–21; *see also*
    insurance
renewable energy 72, 105, 123–4
results-based financing (RBF) 37, 131–2
Rinzin, D. 82
risk: banks' preoccupation with 76;
    broadening distribution effort 120;
    cost of by type **63**, 92, 106, 112;
    equity requirements impacted by
    123; GCF and 120–22; hindering
    investment 61; liquidity 105;
    overcoming or removing 40, 62,
    105; profiles 84; ratings 91; of
    regulation changes 122; in regulatory
    frameworks 110; at startup 42;

uncovered by ECAs 120–21; *see also* country risk; ECAs; insurance
risk cover 62, **63**, 65

Scaling Up Renewable Energy Program (SREP) 145n4
Secretary-General's High-level Advisory Group on Climate Change Financing 139
sector transformation 14, 15, 20–21, 122
securitization of cash flows 107, 110, 118, 122
Seed Capital Assistance Facility (SCAF) 74–5
sequencing of leveraging 85–6, **86**
'sleeping partners' 127
smart meters 91
sourcing instruments 54, **55**
Southern African Power Pool 123–4, **124**
sovereign risk cover 72–3, 92, 112; *see also* guarantees
Special Climate Change Fund (SCCF) 70
'stabilization' investments 127–8
standalone investments 84
standard setting 52
standardization of climate bonds 125
Strategic Climate Fund (SCF) 70
subsidies 60–62, 91, 107, 119
'supplier's credit insurance' 106
supply and demand 63, 75, 102
supply of CERs 28, 36
supporting profit motives 52
sustainability 47–8, 54
syndication 103

tax structure considerations for NAMA hosts 56–7
taxation 1, 56, **57**, 60–61
Technology Needs Assessment (TNA) 17
trade trends 141
transformation 14–15, 20, 83–4

transformational NAMAs 14–15; budget analysis for 81; characteristics of 52; financing of 37; integrating into development 24; ministries involved in 87–8; requirements of 20, 96
transition economies 140
transport 52

UK Department of Energy and Climate Change 69
UK Export Finance (UKEF) 73
'unburnable carbon' 48, 144ch4n6
UNDP 79
UNEP Finance Initiative 39, 93
UNEP Risø 11, 22, 70
United Nations Development Programme (UNDP) 11, 79, 81–2
United Nation's Framework Convention on Climate Change (UNFCCC): Annex 1 countries 3; commitments in 143ch2n1; financing of 67; founding principles of 2, 11–12; funding structures under 70; joint publication on NAMA 11; NAMA Registry 12, 69, 110; Secretariat 12, 29, 31, 36, 87; *see also* Conference of Parties
U.S. Clean Air Act Amendments of 1990 25

Voluntary Carbon Standard (VCS) 64

'working capital guarantees' 106
World Bank: bond issuance 124; green bonds guidelines 78; IDA 111; incentive discussions of 33; inspired securitization model 118; International Finance Corporation (IFC) 53, 74; MIGA 106; Partnership for Market Readiness (PMR) 35, 62, 64

www.ingramcontent.com/pod-product-compliance
Lightning Source LLC
Chambersburg PA
CBHW020002290326
41935CB00007B/273